A Man and His Ship:
Peter Minuit and
the *Kalmar Nyckel*

By C.A. Weslager

Wilmington, Delaware

A Man and His Ship:
Peter Minuit and the *Kalmar Nyckel*

First edition, March 1990
Second Printing, March 2007

Published by:Cedar Tree Books, Ltd.
208 E. Ayre Street
Wilmington, DE 19804
books@ctpress.com
www.cedartreebooks.com

ISBN 13: 978-0-9625563-1-9
ISBN 10: 0-9625563-1-9

Title: A Man and His Ship:
       Peter Minuit and the *Kalmar Nyckel*
Author: C. A. Weslager

RELATED BOOKS BY C.A. WESLAGER

*Dutch Explorers, Traders And Settlers
    in the Delaware Valley, 1609-1664
The English On the Delaware, 1610-1682
The Log Cabin in America
The Delaware Indians – A History
The Swedes and Dutch at New Castle, 1638-1664
New Sweden On the Delaware, 1638-1655*
    and others

The paper used in this publication meets the requirements of the American National Standard for Permanence of Paper for Printed Library Materials Z39.48-1984.

Printed and bound in the United States of America.

Library of Congress Card Number 89-064475

Contents

Maps in Text

These maps are the work of Dan Garrow, member of the art department of the News Journal Company, Wilmington, Delaware. This computerized journalistic technique lends itself to a history intended for popular reading. Geographical features are not precisely drawn to scale in order to orient the reader quickly to locations cited in the text. Professional readers seeking exact detail can readily find the locations on more detailed maps.

Other Illustrations in the Text

Preface and Acknowledgments

I first heard the name of Peter Minuit when I was in the fourth grade of the Mt. Oliver Borough Public School in the suburbs of Pittsburgh. Our teacher, Miss Keehling, distributed well-worn copies of D. H. Montgomery's *An Elementary American History*, which had been used by previous classes who moved on to the fifth grade. Despite its frayed cover and dog-eared pages it was the first history textbook that ever came into my hands; I considered it a rarity.

When we reached the chapter on New Netherland, Miss Keehling told us about Peter Minuit. She pronounced the name like the dance, the min-u-et, and that pronunciation was branded in my vocabulary. I still call him by that name, although I know it should be said min-wee.

"The Indians had more land than they wanted," Miss Keehling read from the printed text simplifying a very complicated issue, "and they sold the island for a few yards of bright red cloth, some shining brass buttons, and some gay beads and pieces of ribbon. The red cloth and buttons delighted the hearts of the Indian warriors while the beads made the eyes of the squaws sparkle with joy."

While writing the above paragraph I copied those exact words from the same tattered book which still bears the faded imprint of a rubber stamp reading "Property of Mt. Oliver Public School" on the inside front cover. Superimposed on the imprint is my name written in blue ink. Miss Keehling allowed me to keep it when I was promoted to the fifth grade, and I believed every word in it from cover to cover.

The account of Peter Minuit's purchase of Manhattan Island from the Indians was not the end of the story. It followed me in my high school classes, and it was revived in a Freshman history survey course at the University of Pittsburgh. Minuit's purchase of Manhattan Island for $24 was as much a part of American lore as the story of Washington cutting down the cherry tree, and the boy Lincoln helping his father build a one-room log cabin on the Indiana frontier.

Four years ago Francis I. "Nick" duPont suggested that I ought to write something about Peter Minuit since no biography of Minuit had ever been written in the English language. He was not aware that I had been fascinated by Minuit many years before by a fourth grade teacher. The idea was intriguing, but I was then busy writing a book for the 350th birthday of New Sweden, and the deadline was getting closer.

"Nick" made a second suggestion. He said that I ought to consider telling the story of the *Kalmar Nyckel*, the ship that brought the first Swedes and Finns to America to make the first permanent European settlement in the Delaware River valley. I had no boyhood motivation to awaken my interest in the vessel bearing this name, which was not even mentioned in Montgomery's *Elementary History*. Of course, I learned about the *Kalmar Nyckel* when I came to Wilmington in 1937 with a growing family of my own.

What subsequently happened was that in 1938 the 300th anniversary of the landing of the Swedes was celebrated in Delaware. I was at Fort Christina Park on a rainy June 27 morning when Prince Bertil of Sweden presented a monument to President Franklin D. Roosevelt in behalf of the people of Sweden. Atop this monument of black Swedish granite was a stylized ocean wave bearing a stone representation of the *Kalmar Nyckel*. I then became aware that Peter Minuit, my boyhood hero who reputedly bought Manhattan Island from the Indians, had been in command of the *Kalmar Nyckel* in 1638.

Thus, when "Nick" made his suggestion I already knew Minuit and the *Kalmar Nyckel*, and when my book on New Sweden was published in 1988 for the 350th anniversary celebration, I had time for a new project. I puzzled over why Minuit commanded a Swedish vessel that founded a Scandinavian colony? Why did he shift from the Dutch to the Swedes? Why was it that most Delawareans had heard about the *Mayflower* and many knew that William Penn landed in New Castle in 1682 on the *Welcome*, but no one seemed aware that Minuit sailed the *Kalmar Nyckel* up the Delaware River 44 years before William Penn's arrival!

The more I thought about these and other unanswered questions the more I began to realize that history may not have given either Peter Minuit nor the *Kalmar Nyckel* their just due. As I dug into the source material it seemed to me that the man and the ship were preordained to become associated in an undertaking that was significant to American history, but too few people knew about it. Too many things happened to be passed off as coincidental, and I formed an impression that the man loved the ship.

Furthermore, I had the sense that his influence remained with her as long as she was afloat, and his spirit was on her deck even after his death. This became the creative concept of the present book, which reconstructs history I wanted to share with others.

An important difference between a historian and a writer of fiction books is that the historian is denied the luxury of allowing his imagination to color his search for the truth. A historian is obliged to confine himself to facts. He is permitted to interpret those facts, but he cannot change them. For example, my title *A Man And His Ship* is not intended to mean that the *Kalmar Nyckel* was Minuit's personal property. He did not design the vessel, nor did he build it, but with loving care he watched over her, and helped make repairs when needed. As suggested in the text, I have chosen to interpret broadly his attitude toward the vessel as one of great respect and affection, although there is no concrete evidence that he ever expressed himself in so many words. But in view of the events that unfolded I believe this is a reasonable and permissible inference. Others who examine the same historical facts may arrive at different interpretations.

A question that readers commonly ask of non-fiction writers dealing with past events and characters who lived centuries ago is where do we obtain our information. The chapter endnotes in this volume will partially answer the question. The reader will readily recognize that primary source material based upon my own research, and that of others, was the principal source. As the word implies, a primary reference is an original source, or the first in order of time. It is of importance because it comes from the same period of the men, events, or ideas discussed in the book. Since there are no oral records from the seventeenth century (tape recordings or phonograph records), and relevant visual data (paintings, portraits, contemporary drawings, etc.) are scarce, written records provide the bulk of the information.

Records in longhand found in archives or public records that have not previously appeared in print must be transcribed, and those written in Swedish, Dutch, or German had to be translated. Such records rarely tell a continuous story, and logical conjecture and good judgment are all part of making tentative conclusions or reasonable interpretations.

This book is not a history of New Sweden – it covers only the time span of Minuit's life and terminates in 1651 when the *Kal-*

mar Nyckel was officially retired from Queen Christina's service. Incidents that occurred in New Sweden which did not involve the *Kalmar Nyckel* are not discussed, and happenings after 1651 must be consulted in other sources.

The reader may question the three diacritical marks above the Swedish letters å, ä, and ö, which also appear over the corresponding capital letters Å, Ä, and Ö. These are distinct letters in the Swedish alphabet pronounced differently from like letters not so marked. If they are not correctly used the word is deemed to be misspelled. For example, the Swedish name for the city Americans call Gothenburg is Göteborg, and the name would be considered misspelled if an unmarked o were used as the second letter.

Numerous references are made in the text to seventeenth-century money, such as the Swedish copper riksdaler (R.D.), and silver daler (D.), the Dutch guilder, also known as the florin, and coins of lesser value. The economic systems of the world are so vastly different today than they were 350, or more, years ago that no practical way has yet been found for making quantitative comparisons between archaic Swedish money and the buying power of modern American dollars.

A book like this one could not be written without advice, guidance, and the cooperation of foreign scholars and institutions. Some helped me with translations; others with geographical information, illustrations, photocopies of documents, or historical interpretations. I want to acknowledge first the Europeans whose names are listed below in alphabetical order.

Professor Alf Åberg of Stockholm; Helena Welin-Berger, Riksarkivet, Stockholm; J. A. Bosmans, Curator, Fries Museum, Leeuwarden; Dr. Sten Carlsson, History Professor Emeritus, Uppsala University; Dr. Stellan Dahlgren, History Docent, Uppsala University and his colleague Dr. Hans Norman; Manne Dunge, Curator, Sjöfartsmuseet, Gothenburg; Jan Folkerts, State Archives, Zwolle, Overijssel; Carl Hendel Friberg, marine artist, Saltsjöbaden; Dr. Friedrich Gorissen, Archivist, Kleve; Dr. Sytha Bijvoet-Hart, Amsterdam; Wilbert A. Hoffstädt and his sister Ferna Hoffstädt of Zwolle; Bengt Sjögren, Landsarkivet, Gothenburg; the Rev. Walter Stempel and C. Parow-Souchon of the Evangelische Kirchengemeinde in Wesel; Folke Ludwigs, Riksarkivet, Stockholm; Marianne Uggla, Statens Konstmuseer,

Stockholm; and E. J. Wollenswinkel, Assistant Director, Stichting Iconographisch Bureau, The Hague.

Among the many individuals on this side of the Atlantic my greatest indebtedness is to my good friends, consultants, and colleagues, Peter S. Craig, Esq., and Dr. Richard H. Hulan. Their combined knowledge of the early Swedish and Finnish occupations, and of Swedish history and folklore, is a priceless asset which they have unselfishly shared with me. The reader will find specific attributions to them at various places in the text. Others to whom I am grateful for assistance are cited alphabetically below.

Dr. Elizabeth Bohning; Gilbert B. Clark; the late Dr. William P. Frank; John J. Goodier; Dr. Charles T. Gehring; Christian Kathke; Dr. Herbert C. Kraft; Marianne Eckerström Mackenzie, Malcolm L. Mackenzie; Dr. John A. Munroe; Allen G. Nelson; Alfred Nicolosi; Allen C. and Elizabeth Rawl; Peggy A. Tatnall; Patricia Thatcher; and Dr. James E. Valle.

I have already mentioned above the foreign institutions to whom I am indebted; those in America whose assistance was of the utmost value to me were the Delaware State Division of Historical and Cultural Affairs, especially Joanne A. Mattern, Deputy State Archivist, and Claudia F. Melson, Curator of Registrations, Bureau of Museum and Historical Sites; the Historical Society of Delaware, and its library staff, with special thanks to L. Ellen Peterson, Curator of Books and Photographs; the Historical Society of Pennsylvania; the Hockessin Public Library; the Library of Congress; the Morris Library of the University of Delaware; Rutgers University Library, particularly Edward Skipworth; the Wilmington Institute Free Library; and the Winterthur Museum Library.

None of the persons or institutions named above are answerable for anything appearing in this book. Their assistance, encouragement, or advice in no way relieve me of the full responsibility for the contents.

C. A. Weslager
Brandywine College
of Widener University

Preface to the Second Printing

In 1990, when *A Man and His Ship: Peter Minuit and the Kalmar Nyckel* was first published, the shipyard at 1124 East 7th Street, Wilmington, DE was a fairly quiet place. The dream of re-creating the tall ship, first mooted in 1938 during the 300th anniversary of the ship's arrival on the Christina River, was slowly beginning to take shape in a small boat shed. The process was not an easy road. To build a tall ship that copies an original from 1625, when there are no extant paintings or drawings to follow, requires money, scholarship, money, leadership, money, contacts, money, expertise, money, supplies, money, manpower, and money. *The Kalmar Nyckel* Foundation Board of Trustees, incorporated in 1986, was first led by the vision of Francis I. duPont and Malcolm Mackenzie.

In 1992 Peg Tigue became the first executive director. The following year, the Board, with Hugh Miller as president and Hunter Lott as chairman, garnered political and financial support from then Governor Tom Carper and several legislators. They gathered information from many sources, such as the Vasa Museum in Stockholm, about Dutch-built seventeenth-century armed merchant ships. The shipyard became busier. They organized crab fests and pig roasts to earn money and built two new buildings in the shipyard. They contacted anyone and everyone who might be interested and supportive of the project from the Swedish Royal Family to schoolchildren. They solicited donations. They hired an architect, Thomas Gilmore, and a boatwright, Allen Rawl. The Board sent Rawl to Central America for exotic hardwoods that would have a far longer ship-life than the traditional pine and oak would have. They chose man-made fibers for the sails and the rigging, again opting for longevity. In 1994 a keel was laid and loft lines were drawn on the floor of the newly built sail loft. The Trustees mounted a membership campaign to provide practical and financial support. They hired a captain, David W. Hiott IV, whose knowledge of seventeenth-century tall ship rigging would prove invaluable. They also hired a blacksmith, carpenters, sail makers, caulkers, carvers, and they sent out a request for volunteers who came in droves. Loans were contracted and more and more fundraisers, such as tall ship festivals, were scheduled. The shipyard was humming.

Frames rose along the keel, boards warped in a steamer and held on by the blacksmith's forged bolts climbed up the sides, carvings to decorate the ship grew out of large chunks of wood, block and tackle and other rigging piled up, fighting tops and masts and spars appeared, a deck spread topside. While all of this was happening, the public was invited to come, see, and learn. This was the beginning of the *Kalmar Nyckel's* education program. As the ship neared completion, Captain Hiott trained his first class of volunteer crew. He expected between fifty and seventy applicants. On the day, nearly two hundred mustered. This was the beginning of the *Kalmar Nyckel's* strong volunteer crew program.

The ship was launched into the Christina River on September 28th, 1997, before a cheering crowd of 20,000 people and was commissioned in May, 1998. The dream was made real, a seaworthy embodiment of the original ship and of Weslager's scholarship. The *Kalmar Nyckel* is among the most beautiful of the world's tall ships and her re-creation is an amazing feat of cooperative endeavor. In a time warp, if the Man, Peter Minuit, happened into the *Kalmar Nyckel* shipyard, he would recognize his ship.

Barbara Mayers
Kalmar Nyckel Shipyard
Education Director

1. Meet Peter Minuit

The freshness of March was in the air as the two vessels flying Swedish colors rounded the capes under full sail and entered Delaware Bay from the Atlantic Ocean. The estuary did not then have its present name but was known as Godyn's Bay, after a Dutch patroon, but the Dutch more often referred to it as the South Bay. The ships turned upstream to enter the mouth of the South River emptying into the bay. This majestic stream is now known as the Delaware River. The crews furled the top sails allowing the main courses to carry the vessels cautiously northward.

The *Fogel Grip*, the smaller of the two ships, probably preceded the *Kalmar Nyckel*; her captain, Andrian Jöransen, a Dutchman in Swedish employ, doubtless ordered that soundings be taken continuously to determine the depth of the water with the lead line. Jöransen had never been in these tidal waters before, and a careless navigational error in an unfamiliar river might have caused both the *Grip* and the *Kalmar Nyckel*, which was following astern, to founder on a shoal. The *Kalmar Nyckel* needed deeper water than the *Grip*, and both vessels were slowly feeling their way through the natural channels from six to seven fathoms deep that ran between the sandbars.

The year was 1638, long before the river was dredged to permit safe navigation. Shoals not visible to the eye were a dreaded hazard to the captains of sailing vessels that ventured into the bay and river. If the *Kalmar Nyckel* had struck a reef or rammed her hull into a sandy grave, the first Swedish expedition would have ended in tragedy, and there may never have been a Swedish colony.

Jan Hindricksen van der Water, another Dutch skipper employed by the Swedes, commanded the *Kalmar Nyckel*, and he was also in the South River territory for the first time. He was no less apprehensive than Captain Jöransen, and both captains were aware of the heavy responsibility resting on their shoulders. As the river narrowed, permitting a view of both shores, they were careful not to sail too close to the marshy skirts on either side of the stream where the nameless tributaries debouched into the river. Today they are known as the Broadkill, Mispillion, Murderkill, St. Jones, Leipsic River, Blackbird, Appoquinimink, Maurice River, Cohansey, Alloway, Salem River, and others. There was always the danger of running into sand bars at the mouths of these little streams that gave sustenance to the main river.

The pines that were first seen along the bayshore gave way to great stands of hardwoods silhouetted against the blue sky behind the stream – white and red oak, walnut, hickory, maples, beech, gum, ash, and spreading chestnuts. It was a land of cedar swamps, and low-lying river banks, green and cool with the richness of the flora. Herds of deer came unafraid out of the woods to drink at the edge of the streams, and rabbits, squirrels, red foxes, groundhogs, raccoons, and opossums were plentiful. Beavers felled trees for building their dams upstream on every creek, and otter families played in the quiet waters.

The waters of the tributaries to the South River afforded a wide selection of fish: bass, trout, carp, catfish, sunfish; shad and herring in season, fought the current in the deep river to reach shallow waters to spawn. Tortoises and box turtles crawled along the shadowy banks where tangled vines were laden with grapes. Mallards, wild geese and turkeys, pheasants, doves, carrier pigeons, hawks, and a host of other birds followed the winding courses of the tributaries to nest and breed as they had been doing for centuries.

Captain Jöransen and Captain van der Water were both impressed, but not carried away, by this natural beauty because they were not sightseers, but had more important things to do. Both had been carefully selected by the sponsors of the expedition for this particular assignment and they were anxious to complete it and get back home. Many Dutch sailors, as well as other sea captains, were then in Swedish employ because of the shortage of Swedish seamen with experience in New World waters. Both captains could be depended upon to remain composed in a crisis, and both reflected the assurance and cool confidence of their leader, Peter Minuit, who was in charge of the expedition. He was also the governor-designate of the colony that the New Sweden Company, with the government's support, intended to establish in America.

Minuit loved the *Kalmar Nyckel*, and like an admiral on a favorite flagship, he made the important decisions and issued orders from high on the poop to the captains of the two ships. But he didn't interfere with them, because he understood the importance of delegating authority, and once he issued a command, he left the execution up to the officers and crews. Both crews and officers looked up to him with admiration and respect, not only as a competent executive, but one who knew the South River by experience because he had been there before. No one knew better than he that after passing Cape Henlopen it was important to run northeast along the west shore, continually taking soundings, and avoiding getting any closer to the land than a depth of two fathoms.

"There's where Samuel Godyn's people founded the Swanendael colony," he might have said in a low voice to Captain

van der Water as they slowly glided past the mouth of Blommaert's Kill, the present day Lewes-Rehoboth Canal, originally named for another Dutch patroon, Samuel Blommaert.
"There aren't any people there now," the captain would
have answered after scanning the bleak sandy shore through
his glass. "That was seven years ago," Minuit would have replied.
"The Siconese Indians burned down the fort and not one
single Dutchman was left alive."
That was the kind of cheerless information it was better to
keep to themselves. This was not the time to remind a nervous
crew of an Indian massacre that occurred in the strange country where they soon would debark thousands of miles from
their homeland.
How did the two ships communicate with each other? That
is a puzzling question because it was long before electricity
was invented and the system of using regular signal flags was
not yet in use. Of course, Minuit could send the ship's boat
to the *Grip* with a written or verbal message, but this could
not be used in an emergency situation. It was imperative that
the captain of the *Grip* maintain communication with the
Kalmar Nyckel if warnings were needed, and the two vessels
were not close enough to each other for voices to be clearly
heard. The writer asked Dr. James E. Valle, member of the
Delaware State College faculty who is well versed in maritime
history for an opinion. The following is quoted from his reply:

> It was quite common for ships of that era to use their national en-
> signs or other flags for signalling. Lowering or dipping the flag
> once, twice, or several times could mean different things, but there
> had to be prior agreement to make the system effective. It is possible
> that the captain of the *Fogel Grip*, sounding ahead of the *Kalmar
> Nyckel*, was instructed to fire a gun and then dip his flag once,
> twice, or three times. The gun was meant to attract the attention of
> the following ship. One dip could mean "shoaling slowly," two dips,
> "shoaling fast," and three dips, "I have run aground," or "the water
> here is too shallow for you." Many combinations of flag dips, lan-

tern showings, and sail strikings could be used if there was a prior agreement between the parties. Bells and drums probably did not figure into signalling between ships, being much more commonly used to summon a ship's company to work, battle stations, or an assembly. That is, they were internal signals rather than external ones.

Another question that has not been conclusively answered is whether or not Minuit landed on the river bank before he reached his destination in order to give the men an opportunity to go ashore. A suggestion has been made that they may have needed to fill their casks with fresh water, which is reasonable, but unproven. Others have said that the ships had been at sea for so long that Minuit believed it would help the morale of the crew if he anchored to let them enjoy the feeling of solid earth under their feet again. The writer has checked into the early source material to answer the question, only to find that an unreliable Swedish author named Thomas Campanius Holm is responsible for first making this claim in a book published in Stockholm in 1702. He said it this way, "When the Swedes came to this country for the first time, they found it so pleasant and agreeable that they could think of no name more proper to be given to the place on which they first landed than that of Paradise Point which is near Cape Henlopen . . ."[1] He does not pinpoint the site of the alleged landing or why the landing was made. Later writers, having no additional contemporary evidence, have broadened the 1702 account to mean that Minuit landed both vessels at a place which Minuit named Paradise Point and which they surmise may have been near the mouth of the Mispillion Creek or the Murderkill.[2] This is sheer speculation and requires more convincing evidence than a vague statement published 64 years after the voyage. Furthermore, Thomas Campanius Holm was never personally in America!

Holm's history was so flawed that he wrote that "Monsieur Delaware one of their [English] captains discovered the river in the year 1600, under Admiral Jacques Chartier."[3] The Delaware river was not discovered by Lord de la Warre; there were no English explorers in the river as early as 1600, and Jacques Cartier (not Chartier) was a French captain, not an admiral, who discovered the St. Lawrence River, and he was never any closer to the Delaware valley than the site of present Montreal! How can one trust an author who makes such errors?

Minuit was not on a pleasure cruise, and if, for no other reason, the danger of trying to approach the shore in anything larger than the *Kalmar Nyckel's* ship's boat would have involved risks that Minuit could not afford to take when he was so close to his destination. One might also reasonably argue that Minuit was unlikely to allow a landing party to go ashore in the environs of Cape Henlopen, or anywhere near the site of the ill-fated Dutch colony, and risk encountering hostile Indians. There was also the danger of prematurely disclosing his presence to the Dutch. He was a brave man, but not a foolish one.

The fact is that the instructions to Minuit, which will be referred to in a later section of this book, and which were written before he left Sweden, directed him to waste no time, but to sail upstream to a specific place on a specific tributary of the South River known as the Minquas Kill. He was anxious to get there with all possible speed because he knew he was in waters claimed by both the Dutch and English, and he didn't want his ships to be seen before he was in a defensible position.

When the vessels reached the mouth of the Minquas Kill ("River of the Minquas") which had been named by the Dutch, the order came, "Bring her hard to port." The crews knew they had arrived at their destination as the helmsmen turned into the stream, deliberately slowing down as the vessels moved against the ebbing tide. The Minquas Kill emptied into the South River on the west shore where the present day Wilmington Marine Terminal is located, about 28 miles south of Philadelphia. The Lenape Indians were then the only occupants of the land having their major villages where the present metropolis is situated, with smaller settlements in present Delaware.

Two miles within the Minquas Kill on the right bank hidden beyond a lazy curve, Minuit found the table of blue-grey granite rocks he was seeking, an outcropping well out of view from any ships in the South River. The rocks made a natural wharf extending into the deep water which was described in an early Dutch account as "a place well situated, as large ships can lie close against the shore to load and unload."[4] This means that despite sprawling marshes on both sides of the meandering Minquas Kill that at this particular deep-river site, cargoes could be unloaded and passengers could come ashore without the need of smaller landing craft. The advantage of having an anchorage in water adjacent to the landing place was only one of several reasons why this site was selected as will be brought out later. Today, due to a number of factors, the water at "the Rocks" is much shallower than it used to be.

Minuit's immediate objective was to secure this location for Sweden, because the rocky wharf extended forward from high and dry fastland where he intended to make the first settlement of a colony to be known as New Sweden. He knew that water transportation would be the colony's only means of communication with Sweden, and the major medium for early colonial travel. A settlement fronting on a navigable water course having an accessible port of entry would be well situated for communication and commerce; the surrounding trees would provide logs for house-building; and the fertile soil would be ideal for agriculture.

Minuit did not have the gift of prophecy, and when he selected this site on the Minquas Kill he did not know he was taking the first step in making possible what would become the city of Wilmington, Delaware many years later. If it were not for the Minquas Kill, the higher land upstream where the Borough of Willingtown was chartered 100 years later, would have been landlocked and would never have flourished. The natural water tie linking it with the Delaware River sustained the life of the borough and contributed to its expansion into a thriving city renamed Wilmington as railroads facilitated the mode of overland travel and commerce.

To the peaceful Lenape (later to be called the Delaware Indians), the site at "the Rocks" had two names, which was not unusual in place-names among the natives, Hopokahacking meaning "place of tobacco pipes," and Paghahacking, "land where it is flat."[5] An elderly Lenape chief named Mattahorn later said he had a wigwam there when Minuit's vessels arrived.[6] If so, he and his people may have been in the woods on a hunting trip, because there is no evidence that there were Indians there to greet Minuit when the Swedish ships landed, although contact with the natives was later made. At a much later date, as the city came into existence, modern residents claimed to have found many stone artifacts in the environs. One elderly informant said there had once been a cave there and within it a spring of fresh water.[7] If a spring was there when Minuit arrived it certainly would have been another inducement for selecting this particular site.

The aggressive Minquas tribe, also called the Susquehannock, did not live along this stream named after them. It was so called because it was one of the routes leading to their country. Their homes were in the Susquehanna River drainage system some 80 miles to the west. Wanderlust and a thirst for conquest led their war parties down the Chesapeake and into the Elk River, and thence to the Head of Elk at present day Elkton. A portage path flanked by Iron Hill brought them overland to the headwaters of the "kill" that bore their name. Then they resumed their journey somewhere near today's Cooch's Bridge where the water was deep enough to permit them to complete the last lap by canoe. Their war parties had been harassing the peaceful Lenape before the Europeans arrived, and hostile relations existed between the two tribes.

When the Dutch fur traders firt arrived in the South River, the Minquas brought their furs down this route to barter with them.

Minuit decided to give the Minquas Kill a European name, and he called it the Elbe River for reasons that he never explained. Not until the administration of Governor Johan Rising, beginning in 1654, was the stream called the Christina River, the name it now bears. The Elbe, a river in Germany that empties into the North Sea, seems an unusual name to give a river in New Sweden, but Minuit was not a Swede, nor a Dutchman like his two captains and half of this crew members. He was a Walloon having a Belgian father and he was raised in a German city. The reader will naturally ask why and how did this non-Swede become the head of the first Swedish expedition to America?

No complete, reliable biography of Peter Minuit has ever been written.[8] No letters have yet been found wherein he provided information about his life, his family, or his career. Despite this scarcity of information about his personal life, he made a lasting impression in the pages of history, and no account of the early Dutch and Swedish colonization of America would be complete without reference to him.

Nothing is known about Minuit's appearance. Was he tall, short, slender, or stocky? Was he bearded or smooth-shaven? No one knows. If he ever had his portrait painted, which seems unlikely, it has not yet been found, and none of his contemporaries left a written description of him. Thus, each of us can see him as we want to see him without fear of contradiction!

The Delaware General Assembly faced the same perplexity on March 9, 1895 when a committee was appointed "to report during the present session of the General Assembly on the propriety and feasibility of commemorating the services of Peter Minuit, the founder of the first permanent settlement on the west bank of the Delaware and the first Governor of New Sweden."[9]

Who was responsible for initiating this inquiry was not stated, but apparently someone who had read about Minuit aroused bipartisan interest among members of the General Assembly. The committee consisted of two members from the House, one from the Senate, and the chaplains from both bodies; namely Senator John Pyle, Representatives John M. Jolls and A. M. Daly, Chaplain W. L. S. Murray of the House, and Chaplain Cyrus Cort of the Senate. The committee delegated the Reverend Mr. Cyrus Cort, D.D., to make a thorough investigation and prepare a brief but authentic sketch of the character and career of Peter Minuit, and especially to discover if a picture of him was in existence. At long last, the state of Delaware through its elected representatives, was showing interest in the man who started the first permanent European settlement in Delaware 157 years before!

After Cort completed his historical research and reported to the joint committee, the committee recommended to the Assembly that a memorial service be held in Minuit's honor at 1:30 P.M. on April 23, 1895. The Assembly approved and services were scheduled to take place in the hall of the House of Representatives. The committee passed a resolution that invitations be issued to the press, to all state officials, members of the Historical Society of Delaware, and "all public spirited citizens in general." One thousand printed invitations were prepared for use by the Assembly and others desiring to invite guests to be present. Today one of these invitations is considered a rare collector's item.

The location was changed to the Dover Court House because of the anticipated crowd, and the joint committee later reported that:

The memorial services came off in the presence of a large and very attentive audience in the Dover Court House, on the afternoon of April 23, 1895. Senator [Thomas E.] Records, Speaker of the Senate, presided. Seated by his side were Speaker [Henry H.] McMullen of the House, Ex-Governor [Robert J.] Reynolds, Chief Justice [Charles B.] Lore, and Dr. Charles J. Stille, president of the

Pennsylvania Historical Society. There were present also in the audience Francis Olcott Allen, corresponding secretary of the Pennsylvania Genealogical Society, Dr. James W. Hearn, president of the Sons of Delaware, with a delegation composed of Richard Fisher, W. W. Smithers, Prof. Theophilus Parvin, William H. Lacey, Dr. D. M. Conner, Warren Harper, Edward A. Price, E. T. Bye, Francis H. Hoffecker, and General Samuel A. Macallister. Dr. Stille was accompanied by the following Philadelphians: C. P. Thurston, Robert C. Cookman, and John Seymour Bioren.[10]

Cort made the keynote address in which he pointed out he had confirmed that Peter Minuit was of French Reformed stock; he believed he was descended from Protestants driven out of France by religious persecution in the 16th and 17th centuries who found refuge in Switzerland, Holland, Great Britain, and Germany.

Cort went on to say that Minuit's people settled in the city of Wesel on the Rhine River in the "Duchy of Cleves," a German province adjacent to the boundary of the Netherlands, and a famous asylum for persecuted Protestants. Also when Spanish armies were devastating the Netherlands, emigrés from the Dutch Reformed Church crossed the German border and joined the French Protestants at Wesel. Cort said that Minuit was born there in 1580, and the family name was pronounced Min-wee, meaning "midnight," although Dutch and Germans articulated the t, resulting in its ultimate modification in modern American English to min-u-et.

Cort did not give the sources for his information except to make a passing reference to the "researches of Pastor J. G. Sardeman, of Wesel, in February 1868." The writer has learned that Sardeman was the author of a brief, undated, undocumented article entitled "Peter Minnewit aus Wesel" ("Peter Minuit of Wesel").[11] Sardeman's questionable data have been superseded by the more recent research of Dr. Friedrich Gorissen, a Kleve archivist and historian, and his findings regarding Minuit are discussed below.

The committee was unable to locate any picture or likeness of Minuit except an oil painting by the American artist William Ranney hanging in the room of the trustees of Rutgers College in New Brunswick, New Jersey. This is an imaginative representation of Minuit as the central figure in a group of Dutchmen and Indians entitled "The Sale of Manhattan by the Indians." A photograph of this painting was obtained and displayed at the memorial services. Cort stated in his address that the photograph would be hung in the Governor's Room as the property of the state.[12]

The original painting is hanging at this writing in a room in Old Queen's, the main administration building of Rutgers University. It was discovered in the university's collection of 1923, but no one knows where it came from nor how long it had been in the possession of the institution.[13]

The face of the man purported to be Minuit in Ranney's painting is reproduced as a small inset in the *Encyclopedia Britannica* (1981 edition, v.6 under "Minuit (Minnewit), Peter." The entry states it is "by an unknown artist," and the editors were unaware it was copied from an imaginative rendition by a 19th century American artist. See photographic insert in the present volume for a photo of the Ranney painting.

As the Reverend Cort neared the conclusion of his discourse he stated that a "noble monument" should be erected in memory of Peter Minuit at "the Rocks" in Wilmington where he landed with the first Swedish expedition in 1638. He added that, "The Diamond State and the Empire State ought to clasp hands in a grand effort to do honor to the memory of Peter Minuit." This sentiment was greeted with resounding applause, but that's as far as it went. No "hands were clasped" between the legislators of Delaware and those of New York, and no monument was ever erected to Minuit at "the Rocks," or anywhere else in Delaware.

In the writer's research for this book, information has come to light about Minuit and his family based on Dr. Gorissen's researches.[14] The data that follows are partially based upon this source.

Peter Minuit's birthplace, the walled city of Wesel on the Rhine from a copper engraving by Wenzel Hollar first published in 1647. Building to left is the old Willibrordi (Dutch Reformed) Church, but the spire is missing having been destroyed by lightning in 1594, later replaced. (Courtesy Board of Publishers, *Weseler Konvent 1568-1968. Eine Jubilaumsschrift, Dusseldorf, 1968)*

Minuit's father was Jan (or Jean) Minuit, a Walloon, born in the area comprising present Belgium. As a single man having financial resources, he came to Wesel, evidently to escape Spanish religious persecution. The Wesel council records indicate that on January 10, 1584, he purchased citizenship in Wesel. He married Sarah Breil, who was born in nearby Kleve, the daughter of an apothecary named Matthias Breil. The couple had a number of children including Peter, born about 1589, and at least two girls, Marie and Sarah. Births were not recorded in Wesel until 1592, which makes it impossible to fix earlier birth dates with any certainty.

The register of the Willibrordi Church in Wesel (formerly a Dutch Reformed Church, but now an Evangelischen Kirchengemeinde (Lutheran congregation), indicated that Peter Minuit (spelled Myniewit) was married to Gerdruudt (Gertrude) Raet on August 20, 1613. Gertrude's father, Arnt Raet, was the burgomaster of Kleve. Her brother Goert (or Geurt) was a Kleve businessman who later succeeded his father as burgomaster. Gertrude also had a sister named Sibylle. The Raets were a landed family having wealth and political influence in this area of the Rhineland where Wesel, Kleve, and Emmerich were then the principal towns. Obviously Peter Minuit made a good marriage in terms of potential financial backers for one having a predilection for organizing business undertakings and assuming the risk in order to make a profit. If he could be described in one word, that would be an entrepreneur. One incident has been recorded where he and a certain Jan Valck entered into a temporary partnership to buy and sell grain, but it was confiscated by the German military. Minuit was forced to ask his brother-in-law Goert Raet to become surety for money he owed his partner until he was able to pay the debt.

Auszug aus dem Trauregister der Evangelischen Kirchengemeinde Wesel

Bräutigam:	Name, Vorname, ~~Familienname, Religion, Beruf, Alter, Geburtsort, usw.~~ M y n i e w i t , P e t e r
	Trautag: 20. August 1613
Braut:	Geburtsname, Vorname, ~~Religion, Alter, Geburtsort, usw.~~ R a e t s , G e r d r u u d t
Eltern des Bräutigams:	-
Eltern der Braut:	-

Wesel, den 07.08.1988 _____ 19 ____

Jahrgang: 1597-1653 Nummer _____

Seite 94 / 95

Gebühr: ___-_,_-___ DM.

Walter Stempel, Pfarrer

Transcript of Peter Minuit's marriage record to Gertrude Raets, August 20, 1613 in the records of the Willibrordi (former Dutch Reformed) Church in Wesel, Germany, now the Evangelischen Kirchengemeinde (Lutheran Church Congregation).

Sybille Raet, Peter Minuit's sister-in-law, married Jan Huygen in 1608, and a son Hendrick Huygen was born to them probably in 1609. The Huygens were also a prominent family in Wesel, and Peter Minuit had a warm and familiar relationship with his brother-in-law by marriage, and a strong affection for his nephew Hendrick Huygen. The latter in many ways possessed his uncle's intelligence, restless spirit, and energy. Both Jan and Hendrick Huygen will show up on later pages in our story.

The Minuits, Raets, and Huygens, like the other Protestants in the lower Rhineland, were deeply religious people. There was a Walloon or French Reformed congregation in Wesel, as well as a Dutch Reformed church. The intermarriage between immigrant Dutch and French, and the native Germans, tended to fragment the population, some going to one church, and members of the same family to another. Both Peter Minuit and Jan Huygen held church office as elders or as members of the diaconate. In the process of intermarriage, Peter Minuit's sister Marie married Gerit Hasenkamp, and his sister Sarah married Daniel Hermer (Harmer). Which individuals were affiliated with the Dutch Reformed church and which ones considered themselves members of the French Reformed church are questions which do not lend themselves to ready answers. The registration of Minuit's marriage in the records of the Dutch Reformed church, probably the church attended by his wife's family, does not necessarily mean he was a member of that congregation. The issue is really of little consequence, because of the eventual merger of the several parishes and the obsolesence of the French language. Today the German language is spoken in Wesel, Kleve, and Emmerich, but according to Dr. Gorissen, "in the 16th and 17th centuries one and the same language was spoken in Wesel, Kleve, Amsterdam, and New Amsterdam."[15] This, of course, was Dutch in which Minuit was fluent. He probably also was conversant in Walloon French.

After his marriage Minuit elected to follow some kind of commercial career which was customary at the time for men in his social position. He and his wife decided to take up their residence in Utrecht, a city in Holland about 75 miles west of Wesel. They were living there in 1615 while he was learning the art of diamond cutting. This must have required extensive training, and was a confining occupation. A man with Minuit's energy would not have been long contented with routine bench work, and he soon became an independent master of the art of diamond cutting. Unfortunately nothing was written about this phase of Minuit's life to enlighten the reader.

Prior to Minuit's move to Utrecht one of his sisters, Marie, who married Gerit Hasenkamp of Kleve, died leaving two small daughters, Amelia and Maria. After Gerit Hasenkamp remarried, the Wesel town council appointed their uncle Peter Minuit, and another relative, as guardians of the children. The relative died shortly thereafter leving Minuit full guardianship of the two girls. On one occasion he was able to prevent an unprincipled landowner from confiscating farmland belonging to his two wards. After his removal to Utrecht another co-guardian was appointed to look after the two children.

In the spring of 1624, the city council requested that Minuit come to Wesel to meet with the members and the two guardians. Minuit replied that he was unable to come because of plans to embark on an extensive voyage. The council in a letter dated May 25, 1624 excused him and assigned his responsibility to the co-guardian.[16] The date is significant because it is indicative the he had decided to leave Utrecht, give up diamond cutting, and turn his attention to the opportunities in the New World. In 1625 his wife returned to Kleve where she and other members of the Raet family owned considerable property.

Minuit was swept up in the great commercial wave that had its origin in the 1590s when Dutch vessels began to ply the trade routes to Africa, South America, and the Orient due to the phenomenal success of the Dutch East India Company. But Minuit did not seek a business connection with the East India Company; he turned his attention to America where he sensed opportunities with the new Dutch West India Company. This brings us to an entirely new stage in his life during which he advanced to a top executive position to the new enterprise. At this time the thought never entered his mind that one day he would be in command of the first Swedish expedition to America. Now, a few words about the new Dutch company.

In 1609, the East India Company employed an experienced sea captain Henry Hudson, to seek a shorter all-water route to the riches of the east Indies – gold, gems, ivory, spices, perfumes, and silk – which excited interest in Holland, England, Spain, Portugal, and many other European nations. This identical quest brought Christopher Columbus, John Cabot, Giovanni da Verrazano, and other explorers to the shores of the New World. Instead of finding an uninterrupted waterway leading to the Orient, they encountered a massive land barrier – the North and South American continents – which stood as an impenetrable obstruction. For many years thereafter, countless adventurers stubbornly searched for a northwest passage that would take them by boat across North America from the Atlantic to the Pacific.

On August 28, 1609, Hudson anchored the *Half Moon* in the South Bay, although at this early date it was not yet known by that name, and was not shown on any Dutch maps or charts. The shoals he encountered in what seemed at first glance to be deep water, made a course upstream seem too dangerous for him to pursue. Moreover, he became convinced that this was not the water passage he was seeking. He left the bay and sailed up the Atlantic seacoast and explored the river now known as the Hudson which the Dutch named the North River. It was not the northwest passage either. Based on Hudson's voyage, Holland, or the United Netherlands, to use an inclusive term that included all the Dutch provinces, laid claim to the land from Cape Cod to and including Delaware Bay and River.

After Hudson's return, a number of Dutch traders and sea captains explored the Delaware and Hudson watercourses. These early voyages were for exploration and trade with the Indians for furs, but there can be no doubt that Dutch navigators had been sailing in and out of the South Bay and River for many years before any other European nation explored or settled it. In fact, as early as October 11, 1614 the name New Netherland appears in a charter for land claimed by the United Netherlands in America.[17]

The Dutch West India Company, modelled after the East India Company, was chartered on June 3, 1621. It was given the monopoly of trade for a period of 24 years in the countries along the entire coast of North and South America, and to the western coast of Africa from the Tropic of Cancer to the Cape of Good Hope, and to all the islands and places from the Cape westward to the eastern end of New Guinea. Within these limits the Company had the power to make alliances with native rulers (which included American Indian chiefs); to establish colonies; to appoint and discharge governors and other officers; to administer justice; build forts, and hire soldiers and sailors to defend its vessels and properties.

Another important objective was to weaken Spain's power by capturing its ships and seizing any gold or silver Spanish vessels were transporting from the New World.

Among the Company's leaders were wealthy and prominent politico-merchants, and it had the support of the States-General, the "parliament" or ruling body of the government. The government bought stock in the Company, had a representative on its Board of Directors, and, when necessary, supplied vessels to reinforce the Company's fleet. There was general agreement among the directors that emphasis in New

Netherland should be given to the fur trade because of the profitable market for pelts in Holland, Russia, and certain other European countries.

When the Company* reached the peak of its growth some years later, it owned a fleet of more than 100 well-built, armed ships and yachts of various sizes, and employed 8,000 to 10,000 people. Of course, as the Company took over the New Netherland, the private traders who had been operating in American waters were obliged to withdraw and give up their activity in the vast area chartered to the West India Company.

The Company was just getting started with its plans to exploit the profit opportunites in the New World when Peter Minuit appeared at the West India House in Amsterdam to offer his services. The executives of the Amsterdam Chamber, the most important of the Company's five divisions known as Camerons (Chambers), were apparently favorably impressed with his qualifications. He may have been known to one or more of them as a result of his mercantile experiences. There were 20 directors in the Amsterdam Chamber, but all of them did not participate in the daily decision-making. The direction of the New Netherland was delegated to a smaller group of commissioners among whom four to six conducted the business. When the writer refers to the "directors" in subsequent references he is using the noun in a generic sense.

The details of Minuit's initial contacts at the West India House have not been preserved, but it seems obvious that the Company offered an unprecedented opportunity for an entrepreneur in his late thirties or early forties to become associated with a young enterprise that seemed destined to grow and prosper.[18]

---

*In this text "the Company" refers to the Dutch West India Company, but "the company" is used to refer to the New Sweden Company to distinguish one from the other without repeated references to the full names.

Abbreviations Used in the Notes

Blommaert Letters	G. W. Kernkamp, "Zweedsche Archivalia," pp. 3-196 in *Bijdragen En Mededeelingen van het Historisch Genootschap. Gevestigd Te Utrecht,* (Amsterdam: Johannes Müeller, 1908). Contains Blommaert's letters to Oxenstierna 1635-1641.
Narratives, Jameson	J. Franklin Jameson, ed. *Narratives of New Netherland 1609-1664.* (New York: Charles Scribner's Sons, 1909).
Narratives, Myers	Albert Cook Myers, ed. *Narratives of Early Pennsylvania, West New Jersey and Delaware.* (New York: Charles Scribner's Sons, 1912).
NN Docs.	A. J. F. van Laer, ed. and trans. *Documents Relating to New Netherland, 1624-1626.* (San Marino: Henry E. Huntington Library, 1924).

NYCD	*Documents Relative to the Colonial History of the State of New York.* E. B. O'Callaghan ed. and trans. vols I-XI. Berthold Fernow ed. and trans. vols. XII-XIV (Albany 1856-1887).
SS	Amandus Johnson. *The Swedish Settlements on the Delaware*, 2 vols. (Philadelphia: University of Pennsylvania, 1911)
VRBM	A. J. F. Van Lear, ed. *Van Rensselaer Bowier Manuscripts* (Albany: University of the State of New York, 1908).
Weslager, 1961	C. A. Weslager. *Dutch Explorers, Traders, and Settlers in the Delaware Valley.* (Philadelphia: University of Pennsylvania Press, 1961).

Editor's note: A separate bibliography has deliberately not been included in this volume because all of the pertinent references cited by Dr. Weslager appear in full in the chapter endnotes. It seemed repetitious to list these titles separately. Peter S. Craig has deposited in the library of the Historical Society of Delaware a comprehensive bibliography of books and papers dealing with New Sweden which is readily available to any reader seeking additional information about the colony.

Chapter 1 Notes

1. Thomas Campanius Holm, *A Short Description of the Province of New Sweden*, trans. Peter S. Du Ponceau (Philadelphia: Memoirs of the Historical Society of Pennsylvania, 1834) 3:Part 1, p. 40.
2. See Map "A" in Peter Lindeström, *Geographia Americae*, ed. and trans. Amandus Johnson (Philadelphia: Swedish Colonial Society, 1925). Benjamin Ferris, *A History of the Original Settlements on the Delaware* (Wilmington: Wilson & Heald, 1846), p. 40, suggests the landing was made at Mispillion Point for "observation and refreshment" which is entirely conjectural.
3. Holm, p. 39.
4. *Narratives, Jameson*, p. 314.
5. Translated for the writer by Touching Leaves, the late Mrs. Nora Thompson Dean, a fluent Lenape speaker who lived in Dewey, Oklahoma.
6. *NYCD*:1:598.
7. Elizabeth Montgomery, *Reminiscenses of Wilmington* (Philadelphia; T. K. Collins, Jr., 1851), p. 117.

8. A biography by Frederick Kapp entitled "Peter Minnewit aus Wesel," in *Historische Zeitschrift* by Henric von Sybel, vol. 15, 1866, is cited by Amandus Johnson and others, but the writer has found it inaccurate and untrustworthy.
9. See *Memorial Services in Honor of Peter Minuit*, a 43 page pamphlet published under the auspices of the General Assembly by Delaware Power Print, Dover, 1895.
10. *Ibid.*, p. 9.
11. An English translation of this article was made for the writer by Christian Kathke, a University of Delaware student.
12. In answer to the writer's inquiry, Joanne A. Mattern, Deputy State Archivist, stated in a letter dated Oct. 30, 1987 that despite careful search she was unable to locate the picture in any of the state holdings, and no one remembers ever having seen it.
13. Alexander Stuart Graham, "The Story of a Picture and an Artist," *Rutgers Alumni Monthly*, March 1923, p. 174.
14. See Friedrich Gorissen, "Peter Minuit und die Stadt Kleve" ("Peter Minuit and the City of Kleve"), *Kalendar für das Klever Land*, Boss-Druck und Verlag, Kleve, 1982, pp. 112-118. The author is indebted to Mr. and Mrs. Allen C. Rawl for obtaining a copy of this publication on their visit to Wesel and Kleve in August, 1988. Christian Kathke made an English translation for the writer, and Dr. Elizabeth Bohning kindly clarified some of the 17th century terms, and sharpened the meanings of important passages.
15. Personal letter, Oct. 5, 1988.
16. Gorissen, p. 114.
17. *NYCD* 1:10.
18. For the beginnings of the West India Company see Van Cleaf Bachman, *Peltries or Plantations* (Baltimore: Johns Hopkins Press, 1969).

2. Minuit Joins the Dutch

A widespread misconception about Peter Minuit is that the Dutch sent him to America as the first governor of New Netherland, at which time he bought Manhattan Island from the Indians for $24 and started a thriving colony. This tale has been told in many textbooks and often repeated in newspapers and magazines. That is not the way it happened, and the story is singularly lacking in historical documentation.

In Peter Minuit's time there was no great urge among Dutch families to leave their comfortable homes in a pleasant land where they had a good living, enjoyed religious freedom, and their country of 1.4 or 1.6 million people was riding the crest of a wave of economic prosperity. There was also a question among many of the directors of the West India Company whether colonization in the New World would contribute to making the maximum profits, or whether the expenses of maintaining a colony would dilute their income. There is little doubt that most of them invested in the Company for the purpose of making a return on their investment, not to transplant Dutch culture to America. It was the West India Company, not the government of the Netherlands, that shaped the development of the colony.

The Company was fortunate that a small group of Walloons took advantage of the opportunity to go to New Netherland to found agricultural settlements. This took place a year or two before Minuit's affiliation with the Company, but since he was then residing in Utrecht he was no doubt well aware of what was going on. As an inducement the Company agreed to give potential settlers free passage to America, and to allow them to go as independent entrepreneurs. They would be given land free of charge if they agreed to remain six years or longer. At the end of that time they could sell their property, or give it away, and return home. If they chose to remain they could become permanent residents of the colony under Dutch protection. During the first six years they lived in New Netherland the Company would decide what products they should grow, and the Company agreed to become an exclusive customer for their crops. After that they were on their own. While they were building homes and preparing their fields, the Company supplied seeds, food, clothing, and farm implements on credit which the Walloons could pay for after they harvested their crops. Strictly speaking they were not Company employes, since they received no wages, but none the less they were beholden to the Company for their livelihood.[1]

If the Company's main commercial interest in the New Netherland was in developing a profitable fur trade with the Indians, why did the directors agree to incur the expense of subsidizing these farmers? The answer lies in the complications involved in doing business with the Indian tribes. Trading posts had to be built where the natives could bring their furs to barter for European trade goods. This was the principal way the Dutch conducted the fur trade, although under certain circumstances traders visited the inland Indian towns, and had to be supplied with small craft to navigate the streams, but having ample space to transport trade goods and return with furs.

This was not a simple matter of doing business with small quantities of glass beads and baubles. Prior to the arrival of

Europeans, the eastern Indians had never seen woven cloth, cooking pots, tools, implements and weapons made of copper or iron, nor any kind of glassware, and the demand for European merchandise spread like wildfire. A wide range of trade items was shipped from Holland in large quantities — axes, hatchets, adzes, knives, fish hooks, looking glasses, gilded chains, finger-rings, combs, earrings, white clay smoking pipes, and other goods. Rum and other intoxicants were in demand, as well as the heavy-weight woolen cloth called "duffels," which the Indian women used to make shawls and skirts, the men tied around their loins in lieu of animal skins, and the whole family used as sleeping blankets. Hundreds of thousands of yards in various colors were shipped in bolts, pieces of which were cut to size depending on the number of skins that were bought in each transaction. There were hundreds of individual Indian vendors who participated in the transactions.

The products used in the Indian trade had to be specially fabricated in craft shops in the Netherlands, and accumulated for shipment at ports of departure. This was a much bigger business than is generally recognized and required an uninterrupted flow of merchandise to America. If trade goods were not available when the Indians brought their pelts to barter, the business would be diverted to the English or French and Dutch prestige also suffered. "Why should we go hunting?" an Indian once asked a Dutchman, "Half the time you have no cloth."[2] An attitude like this taught the Dutch that the native suppliers had to be satisfied in order to hold their business.

Trade goods had to be available when the Indians returned from their cyclical hunting and trapping trips, which usually peaked in the spring. That was when the native hunters came home after a winter in the woods at which season the most luxuriant pelts were obtained. The Indians skinned the animals during their hunting trips, scraped and dressed the skins, and tied them in bundles with deerskin thongs.

During the process of bartering, the bundles were untied and the traders evaluated the skins, often after some haggling with the Indians. The pelts were then sorted by species, bundled together, and consolidated at a suitable storehouse to await shipment to Holland. Although most animal skins were negotiable, top priority was given to beaver and otter pelts, because in workshops in Holland and Russia the beaver and otter fur, which could be felted, was shaved from the skins, then moulded and pressed to make men's hats. There is no evidence that the Dutch traders personally engaged in trapping beaver or other animals — they left that to the Indians. They were essentially buyers and sellers.

The Dutch trader also had to have a supply of wampum beads, known to the Indians as sewan or sewant, either loose or in strings, when bartering for furs. The trade goods usually had to be augmented with a quantity of sewant, to finalize the transaction. The shell beads were obtained from the coastal tribes at Manhattan, and on Long Island. Trade goods were also used to pay for the wampum beads. Dutch currency was not used in the Indian trade, because the Indians had no place to spend it, and they had not yet learned the use of money as a medium of exchange.

One of the problems facing the West India Company was to provide food for the traders, clerks, and other employees in New Netherland who were so busy conducting the fur business that they had neither the time nor the inclination to cultivate the fields or to raise cows and other farm animals. Food had to be shipped to them from the Netherlands and this was not only very expensive, but required cargo space in the sailing vessels that could otherwise be used to transport goods, duffels, and casks of liquor in demand in the Indian trade.

That's why the Company's directors believed — at least during the initial period of developing the fur market — that by placing Walloon farmers close to the trading posts that this would be the means of raising food for the traders and other employes. The development of agriculture was seen as a means of reducing the overhead expense involved in expanding the fur trade.[3] The trading posts, usually situated along navigable streams, were generally surrounded by log palisades mounted with cannon to protect the inventory of trade goods and the accumulated furs. If trouble occurred with the Indians, the farmers could find safe haven in these posts which were essentially forts, and were often so called. They were primarily built as commercial structures, not as citadels to facilitate warfare.

If weather and circumstances favored the farmers, there was always the possibility that they could produce grain in excess of quantities needed in New Netherland, which the Company could purchase from them and sell at a profit in Europe. The farmers might be able to raise tobacco; plant vineyards; and, if lucky, could stumble on mines yielding gold, silver, copper, and even diamonds or rubies. In this event, the mine would belong to the Company, but the finder would be entitled to 10% of the proceeds.[4]

Peter Minuit evidently did not accompany the 30 Walloons who arrived in the Hudson River in the late spring of 1624 on the ship *Nieu Nederlandt* under command of Cornelis Jacobson May, nor did these farmers settle on Manhattan Island whose only occupants was a community of 200 or 300 Indians known as the Manhattes, or Manhatesen.[5]

Captain May, who qualifies as New Netherland's first "governor" settled some of the families near present Albany where Fort Orange was built on the west bank of the Hudson; some on Noten Island (Governor's Island) in the Hudson; and 12 to 16 men and women were transported to an island in the Delaware River known to the Dutch as High Island, now Burlington Island. The exact number of colonists who initially settled High Island was never officially given, but there were not more than three or four families, and they built a small trading post there. They did not build the fort called Nassau at the site of present Gloucester which is approximately 10 miles south of Burlington Island. A fort that far away would not have been of any practical use to them. Some writers have assumed that Captain May built Fort Nassau, but he returned to Holland on the *Nieu Nederlandt* in October of 1624, and we now know Fort Nassau was not built until 1626 as will be shown below.

In 1625, the West India Company sent a new commander to New Netherland, Willem van der Hulst, better known as Verhulst. He was given the title of "provisional director" suggesting that the directors must have had reservations about making him the permanent director. This reluctance on their part proved to be well founded and it had a direct influence on Peter Minuit's career. Verhulst was also referred to as the "commissary," another title given to an individual in command having limited authority.

Willem Verhulst brought a new contingent of settlers with him to New Netherland in January of 1625 on the vessel *Den Orangeboom (The Orange Tree)*. The majority of them had been recruited by the Company from different places in the Netherlands and hired as farmers to receive a regular salary, plus a daily subsistence. There were probably a few Walloons among them, but the majority seem to have been younger Dutchmen, some with their wives, who had been convinced that they would find both adventure and fortune in the New World.

No passenger list has survived, but the probability is that Minuit came to New Netherland on this voyage, not as one of the many farmers, but as a volunteer entrepreneur selected to evaluate the opportunities that existed both for the Company and himself. The line of the narrative is unfortunately broken because of the deliberate destruction in 1821 by the Dutch government of the West India Company papers dated prior to 1700 in order to provide more working space. This has been an irreplaceable loss to historians, but fortunately personal letters, journals, notarial records, and government documents have survived to fill some of the gaps.

One of the useful sources is a semi-annual publication printed by an educated Dutchman named Nicolaes van Wassenaer covering the years 1621 to 1631, in which current events are briefly recorded. Also a few of the West India Company papers escaped destruction, including the instructions the directors of the Amsterdam Chamber issued to Verhulst. He was told to have "his usual place of residence on the South River," and, as the situation required, keep his eye on developments on the North [Hudson] River.[6] The intent of the directors at this time was to make High Island the seat of the government of the New Netherland, but this was before they realized that Manhattan Island was a more advantageous location.

The instructions to Verhulst emphasized that the colonists he brought with him should be distributed to the places already occupied by the Walloons, "but he shall strengthen the population of the southern colony most."[7] Inasmuch as the directors prematurely overrated High Island, it follows that they felt it was to their commercial advantage to have the majority of the settlers placed there. Evidently unaware of the trading house already standing, they instructed Verhulst to erect a "provisional fortification" on the lower end of High Island.[8]

The instructions also contain the following informative item relative to Minuit. The italic has been added:

> He shall have Pierre Minuyt *as volunteer*, and others whom he deems competent thereupon sail up the river as far as they can in any way do so, in order to inspect the condition of the land, supplying them with provisions and arms, *as well as with some trading-goods*, in case they should be able to do some bartering with the Indians on their way.[9]

Minuit's responsibilities included making note of tillable or pasture land, timberland, digging test holes to ascertain the depth of the humus, and keeping his eyes peeled for gems and crystals. Gold was often associated with quartz crystals. He also was expected to make note of what animals and birds he saw, and also collect samples of any minerals that look promising as well as "samples of dyes, drugs, gums, herbs, plants, trees, and flowers."[10]

Although the reference quoted above refers to Minuit sailing "up the river," the instructions are specific that Minuit was supposed to investigate the drainage systems of both the North and South Rivers. As a thorough investigator he would have taken his exploring parties into all the major tributaries, and he could not have escaped finding the prominent outcropping of granitic rocks in the Minquas Kill which would later become the site of the first Swedish colony.

At this early date, it can be assumed that Minuit had his first experience with the Indian tribes on the Delaware and Hudson, winning their friendship with gifts of the trade goods carried by his exploring party. He doubtless used merchandise to compensate the Indians for answers to his questions about mines of gold, silver, copper, iron, or lead, and deposits of salt and sulphur. He was well aware that the directors had asked Verhulst to supply this information.

As a volunteer, arrangements had no doubt been made for Minuit to trade privately with the Indians using for his purchases trade goods in the storehouse belonging to the Company which was charged out to him. At a later date, fur trade was restricted to the Company and its employes, but the instructions to Verhulst in 1625 authorized him to give the colonists and other free persons "full permission to trade in the interior . . . but they must deliver up the said skins and goods to the Company at the price for which we obtain them at the trading-place from the Indians . . ."[11]

In September of 1626, Minuit's account was credited with 6,971 beaver and otter pelts, and some skins of lesser value, which he had obtained from the Indians. The value of otter and beaver skins averaged two or three guilders each at the price paid the private trader, which means that the skins in the aggregate were worth 14,000 to 20,000 guilders. It is difficult to translate this sum into modern inflated American dollars, but Gerrit Fongersz, assistant commissary to Verhulst, was paid a salary of 2400 guilders a year, and Isaack de Rasière, the first secretary in the colony, was paid 1000 guilders annually.[12] Obviously, Minuit had a good head for business, and he must have dealt fairly with the Indians to acquire such a large quantity of pelts equivalent in purchasing power to the cumulative salary that a Dutch business executive earned in six or seven years!

Minuit's reconnaissance of the Delaware and Hudson River valleys left no question in his mind about the vastness of New Netherland, its natural resources, the locations of the Indian tribes, and the opportunities that existed in the fur trade.

In April of 1625, the Company sent reinforcements to Verhulst in four vessels, three of which had animal names, possibly relevant to the livestock they carried: the *Paert (Horse)*, *Koe (Cow)*, and *Schaep (Sheep)*. In addition to stallions, mares, bulls, cows, hogs, sheep, agricultural implements, and seeds, the vessels also brought additional farmers as paid employees drawing rations supplied by the Company. The new instructions sent to Verhulst on the *Mackerel*, the fourth ship in the flotilla, gave the impression that the directors were now less certain about the South River as the main seat of the colony, and the farmers were given the option of taking up residence on either the North or South River, or elsewhere "as may be most advantageous to the Company."

After deciding where they wanted to live and farm, the settlers were to be supervised by a council consisting of Verhulst and a number of others named by the Company including "Pierre Minuyt." Among the council's duties was to distribute by lot the cattle and horses to the head farmers.[13] The inference that can be drawn is that Minuit's activities in the colony had already been observed and approved at the top executive level. This suggests that his future seemed assured in New Netherland if he wanted to take advantage of the opportunities.

Later in 1625, Minuit made a trip back to Holland, possibly to discuss future plans with the directors, especially his role in the colony. It must have already become apparent that Verhulst lacked the qualifications to be promoted from provisional to permanent director, and who knows, the directors may have queried Minuit about this. Minuit certainly wanted to visit his wife in Kleve and assure her that he would arrange for her passage to America to join him as soon as he was certain his future was secure. He certainly wanted to see his brother-in-law Jan Huygen and tell him about his experiences and the opportunities in New Netherland. Doubtless he encouraged Jan to join him because the latter came to America the next year.

Minuit returned from Holland on the vessel *Sea-Mew* arriving in New Netherland on May 4, 1626. When he landed he found the council much disturbed about Verhulst's conduct. They were demanding that he be tried for malfeasance in office. Reference was made to his harsh rule of the colony, and other improper misconduct, although the full details were not recorded.

Sometime after Minuit's arrival the council held an official trial. In a letter written by Isaack de Rasière, the koopman, who functioned as secretary and chief commercial agent, he noted that he was present at the trial. Since he arrived in New Netherland on July 28, 1626, which was less than three months after Minuit's return, the trial was probably held in August. The proceedings of the trial no longer exist, but de Rasière wrote that both Verhulst and his wife were charged with wrong-doing, and sentenced to be banished from the colony. Verhulst threatened to retaliate by making his services available to any other nation who would hire him, and the council added to his sentence that if he ever returned, regardless of his sponsor, he would be arrested.[14]

The council selected Minuit to replace Verhulst as the head of the colony, and Verhulst and his wife were sent back to Holland on the *Wappan van Amsterdam (Arms of Amsterdam)* that sailed from New Netherland on September 23, 1626. Minuit remained as the Company's chief executive officer in the colony. In less than two years he had advanced from the role of a volunteer to director of the New Netherland, a promotion attesting to his unusual executive ability.

This brings up the issue raised in the opening sentences of this chapter. Who bought Manhattan Island from the Indians and when did he buy it? It should be clear to the reader that Minuit was not sent as the governor of the colony authorized to buy land from the Indians. He was preceded by two "governors," Cornelis Jacobsen May and Willem Verhulst. By the time the council put Minuit in charge, settlements had been made on both the Hudson and the Delaware. It is not clear whether or not one of these settlements was made on Manhattan Island *prior* to his return from his second voyage on May 4, 1626. If the island was then settled, Verhulst may have had something to do with the famous purchase from the Indians. Evidence to support this assumption is found in the second set of instructions issued to Verhulst on April 22, 1625 in which the following passage appears:

> Meanwhile, Commissary Verhulst, assisted by the surveyor Cryn Fredericxsz . . . shall investigate which is the most suitable place, abandoned or unoccupied on either river, and then settle there with all the cattle and build the necessary fortifications. And finding none but those that are occupied by the Indians, they shall see whether they cannot, either in return for trading-goods or by means of some amicable agreement, induce them to give up ownership and possession to us, without however forcing them thereto in the least or taking possession by craft or fraud, lest we call down the wrath of God upon our unrighteous beginnings . . .[15]

On the same date the directors issued the additional instructions to Verhulst, they also directed the engineer and surveyor Cryn Fredericxsz to lay out a fort "which is to be called Amsterdam" at a place to be selected by the council when he arrived in New Netherland.[16]

These citations leave no doubt that the directors intended Verhulst to select a site more suitable as the headquarters of the colony than High Island; pay the Indians for the land in trade goods; and then have Fredericxsz lay out plans for a fort and surrounding dwellings. Did Verhulst, in compliance with these instructions, select Manhattan Island and purchase the land there from the Indians, or did Minuit handle the transaction? The contemporary records do not provide the answer, but there are hints that should not be overlooked.

For example in a letter de Rasière wrote to the directors dated September 23, 1626, he said that when he first arrived in the colony on July 28 that "we came to anchor in the river before Fort Amsterdam, with many persons sick with scurvy who are now in good health."[17] Thus, in late July of 1626 there was a fort on Manhattan Island, probably still unfinished.

The vessel that carried de Rasière's letter back to Holland, in which he reported the misdeeds and banishment of Verhulst, also transported Verhulst and his wife, returning in disgrace. When the vessel arrived, Pieter Jansen Schaghen, a Dutch official then in Amsterdam, wrote the following letter to the States General dated November 5, 1626.

This is an extremely important letter, because it is the only known contemporary record of the purchase of Manhattan Island. The English translation reads as follows:

> Yesterday, arrived here the *Arms of Amsterdam*, which sailed from New Netherland out of the River Mauritius [the Hudson] on the 23rd September. They report that our people are of good heart and live in peace there; their Women, also have borne some children there. They have purchased the island Manhattes from the Indians for the value of 60 guilders; 'tis 11,000 morgens [22,000 acres] in

Transcript of Peter Schaghen's letter in the Dutch language reporting the purchase of Manhattan Island from the Indians, as reproduced in Wilson's *Memorial History of N.Y., 1892.*

size. They had their grain sowed by the middle of May, and reaped by the middle of August. They send thence samples of summer grain such as wheat, rye, barley, oats, buckwheat, canary seed, beans and flax.

The cargo of the aforesaid ship is: 7246 Beaver skins, 178½ Otter skins, 675 Otter skins, 48 Minck skins, 36 Wild cat skins, 33 Mincks, 34 [musk] Rat skins. Considerable oak timber and hickory. Herewith High and Mighty Lords be commended to the mercy of the Almighty, in Amsterdam November 5, Ao 1626.[18]

The letter does not name the individual who purchased Manhattan Island from the natives; it does not specify the nature of the trade goods paid for the island except they were valued at 60 guilders; it does not give the date of the purchase, but since it states the colonists planted their grain in the middle of May, the island must have been purchased prior to that time.

When Minuit arrived in the colony on the *Sea-Mew* on May 4, 1626, after his short trip to Holland, he found Verhulst in disgrace. The council placed him in command, although Verhulst's trial was not held until sometime after de Rasière's arrival on July 28. Thus, it is possible that Verhulst may have purchased Manhattan Island before Minuit's arrival as he was instructed to do. Schaghen may have deliberately avoided giving credit to the banished "provisional director" who was in disgrace. On the other hand, Verhulst may have disregarded his instructions, and Minuit, coming into possession of Verhulst's papers when he took command, may have been responsible for making the famous purchase. If so, why did not Schaghen name Minuit as the purchaser of this important island?

J. R. Brodhead, E. B. O'Callaghan, and other early New York historians who attributed the purchase to Minuit, assumed that he was the first governor of New Netherland, and it logically followed in their minds that he must have been the purchaser. If they had been aware of the Verhulst administration, and the fact that two "governors" preceded Minuit, their conclusions may have been different.[19]

However, even if he were not the purchaser, Minuit is certainly responsible for recognizing the commercial value of Manhattan Island as the depot for trans-Atlantic trade and the administrative center of the colony. Having replaced Verhulst, he assumed the responsibility of conducting affairs in the colony to serve the Company's best interests. One of the first decisions he had to make was due to an indiscretion by Daniel van Crieckenbeeck who was in charge of the settlement at Fort Orange. Although the directors had issued instructions to its representatives in New Netherland to remain neutral in disputes between Indian tribes, van Crieckenbeeck decided to assist the Mahican Indians, an Algonkian tribe, in their resistance to a long-time Iroquois enemy, the Mohawks. A Mahican war party supported by van Crieckenbeeck and six of his soldiers was attacked by the Mohawks. Many of the Mahicans were killed along with van Crieckenbeeck and three of his men. This was a critical situation, and Minuit personally went to Fort Orange to investigate. He immediately recognized that the situation might lead to a full-scale war between the Mohawks and their Indian allies, and the Mahican and their Dutch friends.

This would not only put the Dutch and Walloon families settled at Fort Orange in jeopardy, but an Indian uprising could endanger those families living at High Island on the Delaware. He issued orders promptly that the entire civilian population should withdraw and relocate on Manhattan Island, which was centrally located, defensible, and spacious enough to accommodate a large settlement.

Prior to Minuit's decision, de Rasière had already anticipated that the settlers on High Island were not sufficiently protected by the small trading post erected on the island, nor was the island strategically situated to dominate the Indian trade. In his letter to the directors of September 23, 1626, previously mentioned, he raised the question of

whether it would be advisable to erect a small fort on the South

River . . . for the following reasons: First, to keep possession of the
river, in order that others may not precede us there and erect a fort
themselves. Secondly, because having a fort there, one could control
all the trade in the river. Thirdly, because the natives [the Lenape]
say they are afraid to hunt in winter, being constantly harassed by
war with the Minquaes, whereas if a fort were there, an effort could
be made to reconcile them.[20]

The fort subsequently erected on his recommendation was
at present day Gloucester on the east bank of the Delaware,
and it was called Nassau, commemorating the family of a
Dutch hero, William the Silent, Prince of Orange and Stadhol-
der of Holland and Zeeland who was from Nassau. Various
dates have been given to the building of Fort Nassau because
it has been confused with the trading post May built on High
Island in 1624 prior to his return to Holland that same year.
Minuit was in office when Fort Nassau was built in late 1626,
and he was fully aware that its main purpose was to control
the Indian trade on the Delaware with both the Minquas and
the Lenape who, like the Mohawk and Mohican, were also
enemy tribes.

Wassenaer noted in his publication on November of 1626
that "the fort on the South River" was vacated, and trading
was being carried on in the South River by yachts to avoid
expense. In the same entry he noted that Minuit had sent for
his wife to join him in the New Netherland.[21] There is no
evidence that she ever came to America, but remained in
Kleve where she was prominent socially and lived in the
largest house in the town.

In summation, following his promotion to the post of director, Minuit was confronted with a situation that might have
provoked hostile Indians to go on the warpath against the scat-
tered Dutch settlements. To avoid risking the lives of innocent
families, and to demonstrate to the Indians that he wanted to
hold to a position of neutrality in their wars, he transferred all
of the farm families to Manhattan Island; he vacated Fort Nassau on the Delaware and decided to exploit the fur business

there by periodically sending small vessels carrying trade goods to barter with the Indians. At Fort Orange he reduced the manpower to 15 or 16 Company employes to engage in the Indian trade, with instructions not to become involved in any inter-tribal disputes.

Chapter 2 Notes

1. *NN Docs.*, pp. 2-18.
2. *Ibid.*, p. 231.
3. Thomas J. Condon, *New York Beginnings, the Commercial Origin of New Netherland* (New York: New York University Press, 1968), p. 77. It was estimated the importation of foodstuffs was "ten times the expense" of raising them in New Netherland, *VRBM* p. 247.
4. *NN Docs.*, p. 10.
5. De Rasière's letter in *Narratives, Jameson*, p. 103. Jameson spells it de Rasières, but the proper name is de Rasière, see *NN Docs.*, p. 276, n. 37.
6. *NN Docs.*, p. 65.
7. *Ibid.*, p. 40.
8. *Ibid.*, p. 51.
9. *Ibid.*, p. 44.
10. *Ibid.*, p. 75.
11. *Ibid.*, p. 67.
12. *Ibid.*, pp. 243, 199, 191.
13. *Ibid.*, pp. 89-90.
14. *Ibid.*, p. 240.

15. *Ibid.*, p. 106.
16. *Ibid.*, p. 152.
17. *Ibid.*, p. 175.
18. There are a number of published translations of this letter which have slight variations. The one quoted appears in *NYCD* 1:37-38.
19. Charles T. Gehring in "Peter Minuit's Purchase of Manhattan Island — New Evidence," *de Halve Maen* 55 (Spring 1980):6 ff. cites information from untranslated Dutch documents that seemed to leave no doubt that the purchase was made by Minuit. In a later personal letter to me dated Dec. 8, 1987, Dr. Gehring stated that a collection of Dutch documents, including the ones cited in his article, had been found to be fakes. Thus, no documents have yet been produced which can be used as definite proof that Minuit made the purchase, although Dr. Gehring believes that he did.
20. *NN Docs.*, pp. 210-211.
21. Wassenaer in *Narratives, Jameson*, p. 87.

3. Minuit Recalled

By 1628, Director-General Peter Minuit had a concentrated population on the southern end of Manhattan Island of 270 men, women, and children. The majority were farm families, but there were also a few fur traders, clerks, and craftsmen employed by the West India Company. Since all the land belonged to the Company, the settlement was more like a Dutch colonial plantation than a town because none of the residents held title to land on which they resided. Six large farms, or "bouweries" were operated by the Company's employees. The other smaller farms were leased to individual coloniërs (free colonists) for stated periods of time, and they paid rent usually in produce or pelts because Dutch currency was scarce in New Netherland. The Company provided the lessees with wagons, ploughs, farm implements, and a limited number of horses, cows, sheep, and pigs, all of which were still in short supply, and were bred from livestock shipped from Holland. In some instances, Minuit loaned cows to the farmers who fed and cared for them, and sold the milk to pay off their indebtedness to the Company. Milk was used less as a beverage and more for making butter and cheese, always in demand.

The farm families lived in about 30 dwellings, none of which were log cabins. Despite the abundance of trees on Manhattan Island the Dutch did not construct cabins of notched logs laid horizontally one on the other which was not part of the traditional folk architecture in their homeland. A Swedish or Finnish farmer would have built a log cabin which was a common dwelling in the Scandinavian countries, but the Dutch and Walloons settled for bark huts adapted from the kind of wigwams occupied by the coastal Indians. Some builders constructed dwellings by digging a square pit six or seven feet deep, lining the earthen walls with bark. Planks, sawed by hand before there was a saw mill, were used as flooring, and sods covered the roof which was at or slightly above ground level. After the first windmill was built, which operated a circular saw to cut lumber, houses built of boards having thatched roofs replaced the temporary dwellings.

Brick houses with tile roofs were common in Holland, but no brick houses were built on Manhattan Island during Minuit's administration because the limited supply of bricks had to be conserved for use in chimneys and fireplaces. Wassenaer reported that a "counting house" was built of stone, and in the absence of shingles or tiles, had a thatched roof. Minuit probably used this building as a combination office where records were kept of transactions with the home office in Amsterdam, and as a storehouse.[1]

Since the houses were very uncomfortable, especially in cold weather, the ambition of every industrious Dutch or Walloon farmer was doubtless to rebuild at the earliest opportunity along the hereditary lines of dwellings in the mother country. Fort Amsterdam, having cannon in its four earthen bastions, served as a temporary residence for Minuit, as well as for some of the other officers. Although the Manhattes Indians were close neighbors on the island they did not give the Dutch families reason to seek protection within the walls of the fort. Minuit must be given credit for maintaining friendly relations with the Manhattes, the Esopus, and the other Hudson River tribes because he did not abuse or take advantage of them. He observed the Company's instructions that if "any one on our side commits any wrong against the Indians or the natives, he shall be punished as the circumstances of his crime require, in order that the Indians may see that both in civil and criminal cases we do justice without regard to persons . . ."[2] Some of the later Dutch officials were cruel and abusive in their treatment of the Indians which led to hostilities and bloodshed that alienated the natives. So far as the writer is aware nothing like this occurred while Minuit was in office.

To heal bad relations at Fort Orange, Minuit sent Pieter Barentsen, a trader who spoke an Indian jargon and was held in high regard by the natives, to meet with the Mohawk chiefs. Friendship with the tribe was renewed, although the warfare continued between the Mahican and the Mohawk. This was a ticklish situation, but Minuit managed to maintain neutrality, and in the meantime obtain as many furs as possible for the Company from the warring tribes. The pelts were shipped by sloop or shallop from Fort Orange down the Hudson River to Fort Amsterdam where they were consolidated with pelts obtained by the sloops and barks sent to the Delaware River to trade with the Lenape and Minquas after Fort Nassau was temporarily vacated. The exportation of furs was evidently maintained at a satisfactory level, and the directors had no cause for complaint about Minuit's conduct of the business, at least for the first five years of his administration.

In October of 1628, Wassenaer wrote that Minuit sent two ships to Amsterdam, the *Three Kings*, and the *Arms of Amsterdam*, with a cargo of 10,000 peltries and a large quantity of timber. Minuit did not have to be told that the shipbuilding industries in Holland needed lumber because of the scarcity of trees. Oak logs, the preferred wood for shipbuilding, were floated down the Rhine from Western Germany, and also loaded on Dutch ships at Bremen, Hamburg, Lübeck and Stettin,

Königsberg and Riga — even as far away as Archangel. Fir planks used for ship's decks came from Norway and the Baltic, and masts were shipped mostly from Norway. Pine, which occasionally replaced oak in ship construction, was also obtained in Norway and the Baltic. Ship's stores, obtained largely from pines and other timber extracts, came from Scandinavia and the Baltic lands. Suppliers in these foreign countries charged a price which would show them a profit to which shipping expenses had to be added, and Minuit calculated that shipments of lumber from the Company's New World colony on Company's vessels would reduce the cost of shipbuilding. At least it was better to load returning ships with lumber than to allow them to depart half empty if the animal pelts did not fill the cargo space.

Since the Company's financial records have been destroyed we have no information about Minuit's compensation. No doubt he was paid a salary, which was the Company's custom, but he had the Company's permission to hire his own employees to obtain pelts from the Indians which he, in turn, sold to the Company. There was nothing illegal about doing this because trading by individuals, which was later prohibited, was encouraged by the Company in the early years provided the Company retained the right to buy the furs and sell them in the European market. Fur trading was a highly profitable business and the Company enjoyed a satisfactory return as the sole Dutch marketer of furs regardless of whether a salary was paid to its own traders or the furs were purchased from private persons. The key to a profitable business lay in supplying the market with a large volume of skins.

In addition to his commercial accountability, Minuit, assisted by the council, was responsible for combined executive, legislative, and judicial functions in the colony. There was no separation of powers in the political apparatus delegated to Minuit by the Amsterdam Chamber, and no representative government. The council consisted of five voting members appointed by the directors, and two non-voting members, a koopman (the secretary, also bookkeeper of wages), and a schout-fiscal (combination sheriff and public prosecutor) whose badge of office was his silver-plated rapier with a baldric and a black hat with plume. The size of the council varied from time to time, because any of the skippers of the Company's vessels who happened to be in port at a time the council met were considered as ex officio members.

The councillors served in the double capacity, as advisers to the director-general in his executive duties, and as a court of justice over which he presided. The council was authorized to try offenders and impose fines, but anyone deserving corporal punishment was sent to Holland to be formally sentenced. Appeals from the court's decision could be made to the executive committee of the West India Company, but this rarely, if ever, happened.

As the reader has seen, Isaack de Rasière was the first koopman, and Wassenaer notes that Jan (Johan) Lampe or Lampo was the first schout-fiscal. He was an Englishman from Canterbury who had found employment with the West India Company. No official records have been preserved of the council meetings, the judicial hearings, or Minuit's correspondence with his superiors in Holland. These documents were among the West India Company papers that were destroyed, and this obscures important phases of Minuit's career while he was in the service of the Company.

There was no minister at the time Minuit took charge of the colony, but he was instrumental in having his brother-in-law Jan Huygen come to the colony as the storekeeper, and also to serve as a sieckentrooster or krankenbezoeker. This assignment, which has the English meaning of "a comforter of the sick," was a combination lay preacher and male nurse, a recognized ecclesiastical office in the Reformed Church. The incumbent was permitted to hold church services, lead the psalm singing, and read spiritual texts and commentaries to the people, although he was not allowed to administer certain sacraments.

Huygen was examined April 2, 1625 and approved by the Consistory of Amsterdam for service in New Netherland. He probably came over on the *Arms of Amsterdam* with de Rasière, arriving July 28, 1626. He was not the first "comforter of the sick" in the colony, having been preceded at Fort Amsterdam by Sebastian Jansen Krol. The two men worked together for a short time, but since there was no minister at Fort Orange, Minuit transferred Krol on August 1, 1626 as the commissary in charge of the garrison. Krol also served as the spiritual adviser to the 16 or 17 men stationed there.

On April 7, 1628, the first ordained Dutch Reformed pastor in America arrived at Fort Amsterdam accompanied by his wife and children. His given name was Jonas Michaëlius, son of the Reverend Johannes (or Jan) Michielssz, and he was born in Grootebroeck, Holland in 1584, and educated at the Staten Collegie, the theological college of Leyden University. In the college rolls of 1601 he was listed as Jonas Johannis Michaëlius meaning that he was a son of Johannis, but his surname was Latinized.[3]

Michaëlius's pregnant wife fell ill during the long, rough voyage across the Atlantic which lasted from January 24 until April 7, and her condition worsened by the lack of nourishing food aboard ship. She also had the care of the two small daughters who accompanied them. The couple had an older boy, who was left behind in Holland in the custody of a friendly sea captain and his wife. Michaëlius's wife died less than two months after their arrival at Fort Amsterdam. With the two little girls to care for in the primitive living conditions in the colony, the minister needed all the physical and mental strength he could muster.

There was no church building to accommodate Michaëlius, and not until several years later after he had gone back to

Holland was there sufficient building supplies to enable one of Minuit's successors to erect a stone church in the fort. During Minuit's administration religious services were held in a large room on the second floor of a horse-mill built by François Molemacker.[4] This is where the "comforters of the sick" read sermons and biblical verses, and conducted prayer services before Michaëlius arrived, and where the pastor continued to hold services and administer the sacraments. Even before a minister was sent, Minuit made certain that regular devotions were held.

The horse-mill, which preceded the erection of a windmill, was probably designed for grinding grain into flour between mill stones. In the typical Dutch horse-mill in the Netherlands, a vertical shaft was turned by the traction of one or more horses harnessed to it on the ground floor. At the top of the shaft near the ceiling a large wheel was attached which revolved when the horses were driven to follow their circular route. The wheel was geared to other shafting which turned a millstone, or it could be adapted for other uses requiring mechanical power.

The Reverend Michaëlius wrote in a letter to one of his colleagues in Holland upon his arrival, "it has been thought best to choose two elders for my assistance, and for the proper consideration of all such ecclesiastical matters as might occur." He then went on to say:

> One of those whom we have now chosen is the Honorable Director himself [Minuit] and the other is the storekeeper of the Company, Jan Huygen, his brother-in-law, persons of very good character, as far as I have been able to learn, having both been formerly in office in the Church, the one as deacon, and the other as elder in the Dutch and French churches, respectively at Wesel.[5]

Michaelius wrote that 50 communicants, both Walloon and Dutch, attended the first administration of the Lord's Supper, "not without great joy and comfort to many." Only an ordained minister could serve communion, an important sacrament of the Reformed Church from which these devout Christian folk, including Minuit and his brother-in-law, had been deprived for several years. Thereafter Michaëlius held communion services once every four months, one service in the French language and the other in Dutch. Michaëlius wrote that he felt inadequate to preach in the French language unless his sermon was carefully written out in advance, a demanding task for a pastor who had previously served only Dutch-speaking congregations.

Apparently the Walloons believed it was important to have communion services conducted in their native language. Michaëlius did his best to oblige them during the communion services, but at the regular Sunday services, and on religious holidays, he preached in Dutch which he said most of the Walloons could understand. Incidentally, he noted that some of the Walloons were planning to return to Holland "either because their years had expired or else some are not very serviceable to the Company."[6] Among those whose terms had expired were probably some of the families that originally came to America with Cornelis May.

From Michaëlius's letter, one can only conclude that Minuit and his brother-in-law were men of deep religious conviction or the congregation would not have selected them as elders. They not only encouraged church attendance, but set an example by their active participation in the religious life of the colony.

The modern Reformed Church in America is an outgrowth of the Dutch Reformed Church of Michaëlius which had its origin in the Netherlands during the Protestant Reformation in the 16th century. Despite changes in language and ritual, in its tone and spirit it is a vestige of the church transplanted to Manhattan by New Netherland's earliest settlers under the dedicated leadership of men like Minuit, Krol, Huygen, and the Reverend Michaëlius.

Within a year or two Minuit was living on his own bouwerie on Manhattan Island, which he leased from the Company with the consent of the directors. To care for his crops and livestock he employed a foreman and farm hands. Minuit was not satisfied to raise vegetables and the conventional grains like corn, wheat, barley, and rye, but he decided to experiment with tobacco to determine whether it could be successfully grown in the New Netherland climate. He was well aware of the increasing demand for this indigenous American plant in Holland, and other European countries.

Amsterdam was then the biggest staple market for the Virginia and Maryland tobacco leaf, and the center of the world market where merchants from all over Europe could place their orders. Minuit knew that if the plant could be grown on Manhattan Island it would contribute to the wealth of both himself and the Company. The problem was that the Dutch and Walloon farmers knew nothing about raising tobacco, and he hired a runaway English lad from Virginia to serve as a drummer boy, and also to teach them how tobacco should be planted and cured. It was more complicated than raising corn and other grains, and the English lad showed Minuit's hired hands how to sow the plants in the fall, cover them with manure or hay and straw during the winter, and then transplant them in the spring to come up early and mature. After the tobacco leaves were picked it was necessary to dry and cure them to make them marketable.

Minuit was one of the first pioneer farmers to raise tobacco north of the southern colonies where the long summers and mild winters were more conducive to its growth. Nevertheless, Minuit encountered some success, and according to a letter written by Kilaen van Rensselaer he raised 300 plants that yielded 80 pounds of tobacco.[7] Today's visitor to New York's lower east side might find it difficult to believe that tobacco was once grown there in soil now covered with busy streets.

One of the accomplishments of Minuit's administration which is evidence of his sensitivity to the English rivalry for domination of the Atlantic seaboard was his friendly approach to the Pilgrims in the Plymouth colony. This resulted in opening up the trade between the New Netherland and the Pilgrim colony which was then the largest settlement in New England. Founded on the rocky western shore of Cape Cod in 1620, the Plymouth colony was first governed by John Carver who died during the first winter. He was succeeded by William Bradford (1590-1657), who also came over on the *Mayflower*. His tact, good judgement, and executive ability were important in contributing to the success of the colony, and his *History of Plymouth Plantation* is a day-by-day account of the colony by an eyewitness.

On March 9, 1627 Minuit and his council, having learned there were English neighbors to the north of them at Cape Cod, prepared two letters, one written in French and the other in Dutch, addressed to the following:

> Noble, worshipful, wise, and prudent Lords, the Governor and Councillors residing in New Plymouth, our very dear friends: — The Director and Council of New Netherland wish to your Lordships, worshipful, wise, and prudent happiness in Christ Jesus our Lord, with prosperity and health in soul and body.

The letter did not name specific English officials because Minuit did not know their names; his letter was signed by Secretary Isaack de Rasière, "By the appointment of ye Govr and Counsell, &c.," indicative of Minuit's way of delegating work to his officers. The letter as translated in English by a Pilgrim scribe went on to say:

> And also seeing it hath some time since been reported unto us, by some of our people, that by occasion came so farr northward with their shalop, and met with sundry of ye Indeans, who tould them that they were within halfe a days journey of your plantation, and offered ther service to cary letters unto you; therfore we could not forbear to salute you with these few lines, with presentation of our good will and servise unto you, in all frendly-kindness & neighbour-hood.

And if it so fall out that any goods that comes to our hands from our native countrie, may be serviceable unto you, we shall take our selves bound to help and accomadate you ther with; either for beaver [pelts] or any other wares or marchandise that you should be pleased to deale for. And if in case we have no comodity at present that may give you contente, if you please to sell us any beaver, or otter, or such like comodities as may be usefull for us, for ready money, and let us understand therof by this bearer in writing, (whom we have apoynted to stay 3. or 4. days for your answer,) when we understand your minds therin, we shall depute one to deale with you, at such place as you shall appointe. In ye mean time we pray the Lord to take you, our honoured good freinds and neighbours, into his holy protection.[8]

Governor Bradford and his council answered with a letter in the Dutch language dated March 19, 1627 excusing themselves "for our rude and imperfecte writing in your language." They reminded Minuit that they had a friendly feeling for the Dutch "haveing lived ther many years, with freedome and good contente" which referred to the eleven years the Pilgrims spent in Leyden to escape persecution in England.[9]

Bradford expressed a willingness to maintain friendly and harmonious relations with Minuit and his council, and agreed to trade with the Dutch. Subsequently Dutch traders from Fort Amsterdam exchanged sugar, linen cloth, duffels, Indian sewant, and other commodities principally for beaver pelts, fish, and tobacco. As Governor Bradford wrote, "they had some profitable commerce together for diverce [several] years, till other occasions interrupted ye same, as may happily appear afterwards, more at large."[10]

Although de Rasière represented Minuit on a trip to the Plymouth colony where he met Bradford, it is not certain that Minuit personally met the English governor. Nevertheless, he instituted a friendly policy with the English which regrettably was not sustained by his successors. Not many years later relations between New England and New Netherland became so strained that Governor Stuyvesant expected an invasion

from New England. In March of 1653, Stuyvesant enclosed
the city with ditches, palisades, and breastworks in anticipation of an attack.

As Minuit began his fifth year as director-general, the differences between the two factions in the West India Company
became more heated. The basic issue was the question of
whether or not trade could be enhanced by making more extensive agricultural settlements in New Netherland. The
majority of the investors opposed using Company funds to
subsidize such settlements holding to the belief that the Company should concentrate on supporting the fur trade and enjoy
whatever profits would accrue through minimal expenditures.
However, several important directors were set in their judgement that colonization should be undertaken. They were able
to persuade the 19 member executive committee, known as
the Assembly of XIX, that individual members should be permitted to sponsor their own commercial colonies. Their motives had little to do with transplanting Dutch culture to the
New World, or of strengthening the Dutch political position
internationally. Their prime interest was in making money.

A decision was made in their favor by the Assembly of
XIX which culminated in a formal document known as the
Charter of Freedoms and Exemptions issued June 7, 1629.
The "privileges" and exemptions allowing patroons to sponsor
colonies is covered in 31 sections of the lengthy document,
and the main provisions can be summed up as follows:

Grants of land estates or patroonships would be authorized
for members of the Company disposed to establish colonies
at their own expense. The patroon was obliged to select land
within certain specified limits, extinguish Indian title by paying the native owners, and register the land with the Com-

pany. The patroon could then possess the land as a sort of feudal lord with authority to place settlers, appoint officers and magistrates, collect funds from the earnings of his colonists to support a minister and teacher, and do whatever else was needed, within certain limitations, to expand his colony. He was obliged to conform to the general scheme of government framed by the Assembly of XIX and to observe prescribed rules and regulations in his commercial conduct. For example, the patroon was prohibited from engaging in the trade for beavers, otters, minks, "and all sorts of peltry, which trade the Company reserves to themselves." There was one caveat; the patroon could engage in the fur trade:

> at such places where the Company have no factories [trading posts and other installations], on condition that such traders shall be obliged to bring all peltry they may obtain to the island of the Manhattes, if it is at all practicable, and there deliver to the Director, to be by him shipped hither with the ships and goods . . . in order that they may pay to the Company one guilder for each merchantable beaver and otter skin . . . [11]

Despite the safeguards, the majority faction strongly opposed establishing patroonships on the basis that the activity by individuals could result in illicit fur trading. Apart from this, the concept of individual colonization held an element of competition that would conflict with the Company's best interests and result in a loss of income. Nevertheless, the patroons had legal sanction, and the Charter of Freedoms and Exemptions was enthusiastically supported by such prominent investors as Samuel Blommaert, Samuel Godyn, Kiliaen van Rensselaer, David Pietersz de Vries, Albert Conraets Burgh, Johan de Laet, Hendrick Hamel, and a few others.

Some of these men were well known to Minuit. As directors, Burgh, Godyn, and van Rensselaer signed the instructions to Verhulst dated April 22, 1625 establishing policies that Minuit observed in governing the colony. As a salaried executive he was obligated to comply with the instructions of the directorate. Moreover, Minuit himself favored placing emphasis on agricultural colonies, and he found himself caught up in a controversy even though he had not been one of the policy makers. Minuit did not oppose the fur trade, nor did the patroons, but they believed that agricultural settlements in America should augment the commerce in pelts, and would strengthen the Company's commercial position vis-a-vis the English and other European countries. The patroons argued that permanent settlements in contrast to sparsely populated trading posts would deter other nations from trespassing on lands claimed by the West India Company, although at this time no one had the slightest inkling that Sweden would become one of the competitors.

The differences of opinion led to misunderstanding, petty bickering, errors of judgement, and open animosity. No business organization could maintain long-term stability with disagreements at the top level of management which filtered through to the middle echelon. The seeds of Minuit's break with the West India Company were being sown in this bitter climate.

After the adoption of the Charter of Freedoms and Exemptions, three prominent politico-merchants, all then directors of the West India Company, Samuel Godyn, Samuel Blommaert, and Kiliaen van Rensselaer, lost no time in dispatching two representatives to the New Netherland, Gillis Hossitt and Jacob Jansz, to purchase land from the Indians suitable for patroonships. They had already decided where they wanted to settle, and they received advice from Minuit since none of the three had ever been in America. The first tract they selected was along the west shore of the South Bay, and the colony became known as Swanendael ("Valley of Swans"). This is often erroneously spelled "Zwanendael" but all contemporary documents spell it with an s. The dominant figure in choosing this location was Samuel Godyn, then the president of the Amsterdam Chamber. He knew that Minuit had withdrawn the settlers from High Island and moved them to Fort Amsterdam, and that Fort Nassau remained unoccupied. This meant that there was no Dutch settlement anywhere in the Delaware River watershed, and with its commercial potential it appeared to be an ideal location for staking out a patroonship.[12]

Godyn was also in possession of valuable information reported to him by Minuit; namely, that schools of whales had been frequently sighted in the South River. Other Company representatives confirmed that whales entered the South Bay from the Atlantic at certain times of the year and came so close to the shore that harpooners stationed on the beach could take off in small boats for the kill. At a time before petroleum oil was commercially available, whale oil, an excellent lubricant for machinery as well as a fuel for lamps, was worth 60 guilders a hogshead in Holland. The whalebone, or baleen, also had many uses.

If the reports were accurate, Godyn could obtain whale oil in the South Bay at considerably less expense than outfitting whaling vessels for voyages to the Arctic, and sell it at a good profit in Holland. What made the proposition even more attractive was that fishermen stationed at Swanendael could be used as agricultural laborers at times of the year when the whales were out to sea. Favored by good luck he could "carry on the whale fishery in that region, as to plant a colony for the cultivation of all sorts of grain, for which the country is well adapted, and of tobacco."[13] Godyn reached the conclusion that the colony could be self-supporting and also yield a profit without the need to barter for furs with the Indians. He apparently had no difficulty in persuading van Rensselaer, a wealthy land owner and shrewd diamond merchant, and his colleague Blommaert, of the soundness of the investment. Each of them contributed 20% to the Swanendael venture, and later on, Albert Conraets Burgh bought a 20% interest. He had been appointed a director of the Company in 1622.

On June 1, 1629 Hossitt negotiated a purchase of land from

the Great Siconese Indians (also spelled Sickonesyns, Siconesius, Siconese, etc.), a Lenape sub-tribe living on the bayshore. The purchase comprised land eight Dutch miles long and half a Dutch mile wide (a Dutch geographisce mile was approximately equivalent to four modern American miles), extending from Cape Henlopen 32 miles northward to the South River. In terms of modern geography, this was a strip of land two miles wide running along the bay and river from present Lewes to Smyrna at the mouth of Duck Creek (now Smyrna River). It was more than adequate for seating a fishing-agricultural colony, and Hossitt paid the Indians with cloth, metal axes, adzes, glass beads, and other trade goods with which he was amply supplied before leaving Holland.

Godyn instructed Hossitt to register the colony officially with the Company, and on July 15, 1630 he took two of the Siconese "great men" to Manhattan Island where Minuit and the members' of his council countersigned the patent. The document lists Minuit's name as the director and the members of the council as follows: Pieter Bylvelt, Jan Jansen Brouwer, Jacob Elbertsen Wissinck, Symon Dircksen Pos, Reyner Harmensen, and Jan Lampe, sheriff. The spellings of the names are given as they appear in the document.[14] They are spelled differently elsewhere, and this inconsistency is true of most Dutch names recorded in the 17th century. No secretary's name was signed, but de Rasière was being replaced by Johan van Remund, a newly appointed secretary who apparently had not yet arrived at Fort Amsterdam.

Hossitt made a second purchase for Godyn and Blommaert from the Indians on the New Jersey side of the river directly opposite from Swanendael. This was a 16 square mile purchase (Dutch miles) four miles on each side, the western line running along the river in the Cape May area. On June 3, 1631, Hossitt accompanied by Peter Heyes, captain of the *Walvis*, which brought the first settlers to Swanendael, appeared before Minuit and his council at Fort Amsterdam where the second patroonship was registered.[15] Albert Conraets Burgh became the principal owner of this tract, but no settlement was ever made on it.

Having completed the two transactions on the South River, Hossitt sailed up the Hudson River to Fort Orange, and acting principally in van Rensselaer's behalf, bought land from the Indians on July 27, 1630. This land extended the previous purchases made by Bastiaen Jansen Krol for van Rensselaer and in its totality represented another patroonship called Rensselaerswyck, lying on both sides of the Hudson above and below Fort Orange. See Map 1. On August 13, 1630, Minuit registered this purchase at Fort Amsterdam, and the document bore the signatures of the same council members appearing on the registration for the Swanendael tract previously cited. Remund, the new secretary, was still absent, and the document was signed by "Lenart Cole, Deputy Secretary," and written in his own hand.[16]

Minuit, acting in behalf of the patroons, bought Staten Island from the Indians in 1630 for "Duffels, Kittles, Axes, Hoes, Wampum, Drilling Awls, Jews Harps, and diverse other small wares."[17] This tract, along with adjacent purchases, became part of the patroonship called Pavonia owned by Michiel Pauw extending along the west side of the Hudson from the Narrows to Hoboken, including Staten Island.[18]

Much more could be written about the other patroonships, but enough evidence has been presented to show that Minuit, by virtue of his position as the Company's chief executive officer in New Netherland, was responsible for corroborating that the lands had been bought from the Indians and paid for, and for formally registering each patroonship. Quite naturally his willing involvement left no doubt that he cooperated closely with the patroons, and was, in fact, supportive of their interests. This alienated him from the anti-patroon faction in the Company and was at the root of the dissension that developed.

The friction was aggravated in June of 1631 when six new

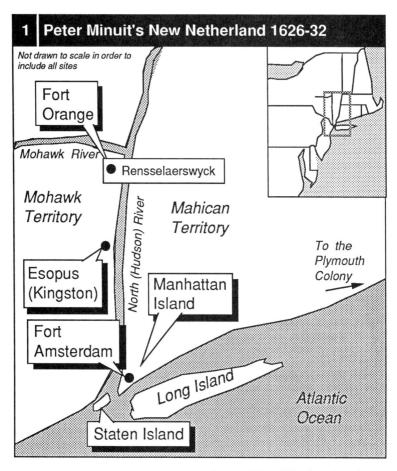

1 Peter Minuit's New Netherland 1626-32

Not drawn to scale in order to include all sites

Fort Orange

Mohawk River

● Rensselaerswyck

Mohawk Territory

North (Hudson) River

Mahican Territory

To the Plymouth Colony →

Esopus (Kingston)

Manhattan Island

Fort Amsterdam

Long Island

Atlantic Ocean

Staten Island

"Mahican Territory" was the homeland of the "Mahikanders," the Indians who greeted Henry Hudson in 1609 when he first sailed up the river now bearing his name. Not to be confused with the Mohegans of coastal Connecticut.

members were elected to the Amsterdam Chamber to replace those who had served in office for the staggered six year terms. Among these was Marcus de Vogelaer an outspoken opponent of the patroon system, and he was able to influence the others; from 1631 to 1633 the Company pursued an anti-patroon policy.[19]

Other problems arose on Manhattan Island which in some

modern corporate organizations fester from what are termed "office politics," and the motives seemed to be to unseat the boss, namely Minuit, in order to please the anti-patroon faction in Holland. From the scanty information that has been unofficially recorded in letters written by van Rensselaer and others, it appears that the new secretary, Johan Remund, started the trouble, because he was on the opposite side of the patroon question from Minuit. He did his best to ingratiate himself with de Vogelaer and others in power, for his own selfish reasons. Sijmon Dircksen Pos, a member of Minuit's council, said in a letter dated September 16, 1630 that van Remund and Minuit "are very much embittered against one another," and as a result of their differences that the Company's interests and business were being neglected. It is not difficult to understand how a personality clash and discord at the management level of the colony would have a negative effect on the morale of the subordinates and would inevitably be reflected in a decline in productivity.

In the same letter Pos wrote that:

> The minister, Jonas Michielsz, is very energetic here stirring up the fire between them; he ought to be a mediator in God's church and community but seems to me to be the contrary. The honorable directors hear nothing but idle complaints from their subjects; one says this, the other that, so that in place of the Company's servants looking after the trading, some one else in the meanwhile goes off with the skins.[20]

The Reverend Michaëlius was in fact fomenting trouble, and in a letter dated September 13, 1630, he wrote to Joannes van Foreest, a state official living in Hoorn, complaining that his Christian labors were suffering "through a nefarious enterprise of wicked men, who have created tragedies among us." He focused criticism on Minuit calling him dishonest and wicked; unworthy of his office; a cruel oppressor of the innocent; and accusing him and the members of his council of cheating the Company for their own profit.

He added that he had written the directors in Amsterdam about the situation, and when it became known in the colony that he had gone over Minuit's head that "the governor tried to silence me and make me hated, in the meantime through secret complaints by [to?] the Lords of the Company, and at last has tried to eject me out of this place, branded with the mark of shame."[21]

What happened to cause this backbiting toward the man the minister had favored as an elder in the church, and was still holding this position, still remains unexplained. Michaëlius submitted no evidence for his slanderous charges, the most serious of which was that the director and his council were cheating the Company. The minister had nothing to do with the management of the colony and was not privy to business correspondence between Minuit and the directors, nor with their instructions to him. He did not normally see the bookkeeping records which were available to van Remund, and Remund may have given him misinformation to prejudice him against Minuit.

What we have on which to make a judgment are ugly charges unsupported by facts made in a personal letter in which the minister claimed that Minuit "plots indefatigably to disperse all the fruits of my ministry and of my labors."[22] Certainly this was not in keeping with the character of a man recognized by his contemporaries as a devout Christian.

Van Rensselaer, a prolific letter writer who was party to the crossfire of letters from New Netherland, came to the conclusion that van Remund, whom he personally knew, was at the bottom of the trouble in the colony. He referred to him as "this false secretary, who has slandered many men behind their backs."[23]

In the absence of concrete evidence it is impossible more than 350 years later to sit in judgment on this dispute. Minuit may not have been immune from criticism, but the record is clear that he had served satisfactorily as the Company's ranking officer in New Netherland for almost six years before the wrangling began. During this time he displayed competency or the directors would certainly have replaced him, or his council would have unseated him as they did Verhulst. As the reader has seen his accomplishments speak for themselves; he protected the colony against Indian attack by bringing the families together and concentrating the population where a metropolis ultimately grew, and which still remains as the great natural pier in the commerce world. He maintained a neutral position with the Indians and established commerce with the Pilgrims. While he was in office the following pelts were exported from New Netherland to Holland.[24]

Year	Beavers	Otters, etc.	Value-guilders
1626	7,258	857	45,050
1627	7,520	370	12,730
1628	6,951	734	61,075
1629	5,913	681	62,185
1630	6,041	1,085	68,012
1631	(figures unavailable)		
1632	13,513	1,661	143,125
TOTAL (Combined)	52,584 pelts		392,177

Admittedly these figures are a sad commentary on the ruthless destruction of animal life in America, but that is an issue to be debated at another time. In terms of complying with his orders, these pelts represented an unprecedented source of income for Minuit's employers. Figures are not available on the quantities of lumber and tobacco from Virginia and elsewhere which Minuit also shipped to Holland, but the volume was a substantial contribution to the Company.

In view of the personality clashes reported from New Netherland, and the slanderous statements they had received, the directors were less concerned about the imports in the past than they were about the present and future state of the business. As hard-headed businessmen, it was apparent that the time had come for a shakeup in the organization and the best way to get to the bottom of the situation was to summon the principals to report to Amsterdam for interrogation.

The instructions sent to Minuit came on the vessel *Eendracht* (which ironically translates as *Unity*) carried by the Company's emissary Coenraet Notelman who left Holland for America shortly after July 7, 1631. The main thrust of the message was that Minuit, van Remund, Jan Lampe, the Reverend Michaëlius, Peter Blyvelt, Gerrit Mattheusz de Reux, farm manager, and others involved in the controversy should return to Amsterdam promptly on the *Eendracht* for questioning. Notelman was to remain at Fort Amsterdam as a replacement for Lampe so that the colony would not be deprived of a schout-fiscal during the investigation. Bastian Jansen Krol, Minuit's trusted commander at Fort Orange, received orders to take charge at Manhattan on what appeared to be a provisional basis, presumably until Minuit returned. Krol was glad to get back to the heart of the colony, which he preferred to his assignment at Fort Orange.

There must have been considerable excitement as well as uneasiness in preparing for the voyage, and Minuit ordered that all the pelts in the storehouse be made ready for shipment. Even though Michaëlius had accused him of not paying sufficient attention to the Indian trade, the cargo of furs was an exceptionally large one. En route to Holland, the *Eendracht* with its suspensive passengers, including women and children, "laden with peltries" was held up in Plymouth, England on April 5, 1632. The English authorities claimed that the Dutch West India Company was illegally engaged in the fur trade in territory that belonged to England. Messages flew back and forth across the English channel on speedy sailboats between the West India Company, the States General, and Holland's ambassador in London.

The English authorities fell back on the first Virginia charter passed under the Great Seal of England on April 10, 1606
in which the term "Virginia" was used to designate the full
sweep of the North American coast that lay above Spanish
Florida. The Dutch diplomats protested that there was no English settlement in New Netherland, and that Minuit's people
were well within their rights to trade with the Indians. Minuit
and Jan Lampe became involved in trying to persuade the
English to release the vessel in order to deliver the pelts to
Amsterdam, but the *Eendracht* remained at anchor in
Plymouth more than a month later as the diplomats were still
arguing. Even King Charles I of England was persuaded to
give an audience to representatives of the Dutch government.[25]

This was Minuit's first exposure to international power
politics and he must have been impressed with English logic
and stubbornness in the dispute over ownership of land in
America. This subject, which is beyond the scope of the
present account, remained a sore issue between England and
the Netherlands, and eventually England seized the Dutch
territory in a coup in 1664.

Late in May of 1632 the English agreed to release the
Eendracht. Minuit and his entourage had already left
Plymouth on another vessel to face the directors in Amsterdam. Nothing is said about Minuit's wife in any of the letters
or extant records — not one single word.

Neither are there any records of the hearing held by the
directors, how it was conducted, the names of the testifiers or
the questioners, nor the nature of the testimony. Certain as-
sumptions can be made based on the fact that the Company
was under severe criticism at the time of the recall of Minuit
and his associates for having incurred unnecessary expenses
in the American venture. Among the alleged extravagances
in New Netherland were:

> building the ship *New Netherland* at an excessive outlay, by erecting
> three expensive mills, by brick-making, by tar-burning, by ash-burn-

ing, by salt-making and the like operations, which through bad management and calculation have all gone to nought or come to little, but which nevertheless have cost much. Had the same money been used in bringing people and importing cattle, the country would now have been of great value.[26]

Doubtless Minuit bore the brunt of the criticism, and some of it may have been justified, but it is unfair to censure him for not bringing more people and cattle to New Netherland when that is precisely what he favored and the anti-patroon faction opposed. He was not responsible for the policies made by the Company which he presumably implemented to the best of his ability. He cannot be blamed because the population of the New Netherland remained static — the decision whether or not to send settlers did not rest with him on Manhattan Island, but was made in the West India House in Amsterdam.

Building the vessel *New Netherland* appears to have been a bold effort to enrich the Company, not to impoverish it. The important objective of raiding Spanish vessels remained paramount, and to seize Spain's so-called Silver Fleet was the dream of the Company's directors and every privateer in northern Europe. To the Dutch government the capture of Spanish vessels was condoned and encouraged as a lawful undertaking.

At intervals, Spanish ships carrying gold and silver from the mines in Mexico and Panama converged in Havana to form the convoy which became known as the Silver Fleet. In mid-November of 1628 the Dutch admiral Pieter Heyn, with a formidable attacking force, captured the fleet of 20 Spanish vessels loaded with gold, silver, and other merchandise in Matanzas Bay. This wealth enabled the Company to pay all of its outstanding debts and to distribute extra dividends to the stockholders.[27] Undoubtedly this influenced Minuit's thinking, not in terms of seizing the whole Spanish fleet again, but in picking off individual Spanish prizes sailing with less than adequate military protection. If the cargo turned out to be sugar, not gold or silver, it, too, was desirable booty because no sugar was growing in New Netherland, and it was also in demand in Holland.

It is uncertain who conceived of building the vessel but the work was supervised by two experienced Walloon shipbuilders who came to Fort Amsterdam. Instead of exporting timber to Holland for shipbuilding, the concept of building a vessel in America from trees growing in the colony appealed to Minuit and he encouraged the project, allocating funds and manpower to support it.

In July of 1630 when Gillis Hossitt sailed up the Hudson to buy land from the Indians for van Rensselaer, he encountered a party of workmen in a logging camp where they were cutting down trees to finish the ship at Manhattan. On September 16, 1630, Symon Dircksen Pos wrote to van Rensselaer from Fort Amsterdam with the news that the new ship was still under construction, but the builders had to stop work temporarily to protect it from damage that might be done to it "by the strong ice drift we are having."[28] By 1631, the *New Netherland* had been launched, a powerful vessel of from 600 to 800 tons burden carrying 30 cannon. This was heavy armament for a merchant ship, and more than adequate to intimidate Spanish prizes. There is little question that leaders in the Amsterdam Chamber approved because Minuit would not have independently engaged in a project of this magnitude without their endorsement.

Next to nothing is known about the voyages of the *New Netherland* and one has the feeling that the directors may have believed the less said about her the better. Several clues about her role as a sea rover are given in the journal of David Pietersz de Vries, a Dutch merchant, seaman, adventurer, and patroon. On July 12, 1632 de Vries, in command of the *Walvis (Whale)* enroute to Swanendael, encountered the *New Netherland* in the waters off the Isle of Wight. He refers to her by name and describes her as "a large ship, which was built in New Netherland which was bound for the West Indies, whither

I had good company." In other words, if he were accompanied by the *New Netherland*, he was assured of adequate protection from an attack by privateers or pirates as long as he was in her company. The two vessels sailed together laying a course for the Canary Islands where favorable trade winds would be encountered for the Atlantic crossing.

Late on August 13 they encountered a Turkish vessel which apparently was looking for its own prizes, and to the Dutch, Turkish ships were fair prey. But as the Turkish vessel approached the *Walvis* the captain saw she was accompanied by the *New Netherland* and he quickly turned away. The captain of the *New Netherland*, thinking the Turkish ship would be a worthwhile prize, took off after her as night fell.

The *Walvis* continued alone on her course toward the Leeward Island in the Caribbean, and from there she sailed to the South River. En route, de Vries encountered the *New Netherland* at St. Vincent and again at St. Martin. Although he discreetly gives no details about her mission, one gathers the impression that he did not want to enter in his journal that the Company was using her both as a merchant ship and a sea rover in search of Spanish prizes.[29] Is it not ironical that at the very time Minuit was facing a board of inquiry at Amsterdam questioning his devotion to duty that the ship built in New Netherland during his administration was seeking wealth to contribute to the treasury of the West India Company?

All of the charges were aired during the directors' inquisition of Minuit and those members of his staff who accompanied him, and when everything was over "the false secretary," Johan van Remund, emerged as a victor in the controversy with the full support of the anti-patroon faction. He was the only one who was authorized to return to Fort Amsterdam and resume his official position as the koopman. Jan Lampe had already been replaced by Notelman as schout-fiscal, and the records available to the writer do not explain what happened to Lampe. But van Rensselaer wrote that Bylvelt and de Reux "were prevented from returning thither," which can only be interpreted to mean they were banned from New Netherland as Verhulst had been interdicted almost a decade before.

Since Michaëlius was not a political appointee it is not certain that he testified at the hearing, but if so he doubtless spoke against Minuit. It is a matter of record that he was summoned before the Consistory at Amsterdam to make an independent report. The Consistory was a religious body subordinate to the Classis of Amsterdam, and the minutes of the Consistory dated March 4, 1632 indicated that he made his report there, probably in advance of the Company's enquiry. The minutes briefly state that he

> gave a detailed account of what happened to him in this place [New Netherland] and also about the ministration of his service, in the time of his office. Relating in particular what had taken place between him and the governor, being different kinds of incidents which had happened, whereby his service and person have been subjected to many disturbances and troubles. The council having heard and understood all this, has welcomed his person in a friendly manner, and with thanks for his services he departed.[30]

Not one word about his specific accusations! No details or evidence to support the charges made in his letters!

During the next five years nothing is known about Michaëlius's activities, but his name came up again in 1637 when he was living in Holland, then aged 53. At that time he evidently did not have a church assignment. The West India Company was in need of a minister to go to New Netherland, and Michaëlius was willing to return to America. The Classis of Amsterdam requested the Amsterdam Chamber of the Company to approve of him, and one would think that his long experience in the pulpit and his four years service in New Netherland would have made him a logical candidate. Nevertheless, an evasive answer was given "that when they had need of him they would summon him." The Classis renewed the request, but the Amsterdam Chamber "gave little or no hope." When the Classis requested a more definite reply, the blunt answer came back that Michaëlius had been rejected by the Assembly of XIX, which was unusual because decisions like this were normally made at a lower level.[31] The Assembly of XIX gave no reason — perhaps it was not forgotten how the minister had prejudiced Governor Minuit in the latter days of the administration.

The inquiry at Amsterdam brought an end to Minuit's employment by the West India Company, and Bastian Jansen Krol remained in charge in New Netherland until Wouter van Twiller, a nephew of Kiliaen van Rensselaer, was appointed to succeed him in July of 1632.[32] Evidence is lacking that Minuit was discharged, nor can it be said that he resigned, and nothing in the record indicates that he was prohibited from returning to the New Netherland as a private entrepreneur. To some historians it may appear unlikely that the directors would have summarily discharged him, because he still had supporters among the members of the directorate despite the anti-patroon faction. After all, it was common knowledge that he had been a competent executive with an unblemished record until he became the victim of personality clashes during his last year in office that cast shadows on his character.

Others may believe that the anti-patroon faction callously voted him out of office to get rid of him. There is also a third reasonable possibility; his separation from the Company could have been by mutual agreement, perhaps with some kind of terminal pay. In the absence of facts no one really knows.

In the late summer of 1632, embittered against the Company, Minuit was without a job. Fortunately he had accumulated moderate savings as a salaried employe and private entrepreneur, a permissible way of life among both government and West India Company officials in the 17th century. He was not a wealthy man, but neither was he a poor one.

Chapter 3 Notes

1. Wassenaer in *Narratives, Jameson*, pp. 83, 88.
2. *NN Docs.*, pp. 112-113.
3. A. Eekhof, *Johnas Michaëlius Founder of the Church in New Netherland* (Leyden: A. W. Sitjhoff's Publishing Company, 1926), p. 17. For a popular account see J. J. Ferdinand van Melle, "In Search of Jonas Michaëlius" *de Halve Maen*, 53, no. 3, Fall 1978, pp. 1, ff.
4. *Narratives, Jameson*, p. 83.
5. Michaëlius letter, Aug. 11, 1628, *ibid.*, p. 124.
6. *Ibid.*, p. 125.
7. *VRBM*, p. 219.
8. *Bradford's History of Plymouth Plantation*, (Boston: Wright & Potter, 1894), pp. 268-269.
9. *Ibid.*, pp. 270-271.
10. *Ibid.*, p. 271.
11. *Narratives, Jameson*, pp. 90-96 for full text of the Charter of Freedoms and Exemptions; cf. *VRBM* pp. 136-152.
12. See "The Swanendael Tragedy," chapter 4, *Weslager, 1961*.
13. De Vries (1630) in *Narratives, Myers*, p. 8.
14. *NYCD* 1:43. See *Weslager, 1961*, pp. 258-259 for transcript of June 1, 1629 Indian sale to Hossitt.

15. *NYCD* 12:17-18.
16. *NYCD* 1:44. cf. *VRBM*, pp. 181-183.
17. Cornelius Melyen's deposition, January 30, 1659 in *Collections, N.Y. Hist. Soc.* 46 (1913) p. 124.
18. *NYCD* 13:2.
19. *Peltries or Plantations*, pp. 120-121.
20. *VRBM*, pp. 169-170.
21. Eekhof, p. 69.
22. *Ibid.*
23. *VRBM*, p. 269.
24. *Collections, N.Y. Hist. Soc.*, 2nd series, 1 (1841), p. 385.
25. *NYCD* 1:45 passim.
26. "Representation of New Netherland" (1650), *Narratives, Jameson*, p. 321.
27. *Pelts or Plantations*, pp. 26, 45, 106, 117, 120.
28. For information about the ship *New Netherland*, see *VRBM*, p. 169 (1630); *Narratives, Jameson* (1650), p. 321. Cf. James Grant Wilson, *The Memorial History of the City of New York.*, 4 vols., (New York, 1892), 1:163, 168.
29. De Vries (1632) in *Narratives, Myers*, pp. 10, 11, 12. See also "Dutch and English on the Hudson," the *Chronicle of America Series*, ed. Allen Johnson 7 (Yale University Press, New Haven, 1921), pp. 55-56.
30. Eekhof, p. 73.
31. *Ibid.*, p. 74.
32. A complete list of governors of New Netherland is given as follows in *Narratives, Jameson*, p. 66:
    Cornelis Jacobsen May, 1624-1625
    Willem Verhulst, 1625-1626
    Peter Minuit, 1626-1632
    Sebastian Jansen Krol, 1632-1633
    Wouter van Twiller, 1633-1638
    Willem Kieft, 1638-1647
    Peter Stuyvesant, 1647-1664

4. A Swedish Connection

Before Wouter van Twiller left Amsterdam to take over the director's post from Bastian Jansen Krol, Minuit met with him and van Rensselaer to sell them the livestock and tools left behind on his bouwerie on Manhattan Island. Van Twiller intended to continue the farm that Minuit operated, and van Rensselaer was eager to buy any excess animals and have them shipped up the Hudson to his colony at Fort Orange where livestock was scarce. Minuit signed an agreement on July 20, 1632 after his arrival in Holland confirming the transfer of his property to the two Dutchmen. The contents of the document may appear to be insignificant, but his writings are so scarce that some insight may be revealed about his character by noting his attention to small details. The following appears in his handwriting:[1]

> four old mares, with colt at the time
> four old cows, also with calf
> two heifers, then one year old
> six sheep
> six hogs
> These sheep and hogs Minuit did not receive from the Company; van Twiller must claim them therefore of the Company or deduct from the horses and cows which he must hereafter furnish to the same.

a goodly number of chickens and pigeons
a half worn wagon
an old ditto
two plows with their belongings
about 15 morgens [approx. 30 acres] of winter seeding;
also seed ordered and directed sown as follows:
    three morgens of oats
    one morgan of peas
a well seeded and planted garden

In terms of a modern farm, or even a truck garden, this list does not appear impressive, but livestock was very scarce at the time because of the difficulty in bringing the animals from Holland in sailing ships. Many did not survive the long voyage on the rolling vessels, and others could not adjust to the new American environment after their arrival.

This was an age before mechanical farm equipment was known; the earth was turned over by horse-drawn hand plows, cultivated with hoes and wood rakes, and the corn and grain crops harvested by sickle or scythe. Farming was laborious work, and the cultivated area was necessarily small on each bouwerie due to the limited number of hired hands. In dry seasons water had to be carried to the fields in wooden buckets, and in wet seasons horses and wagons were in danger of being bogged down in the mire.

In the hard bargain Minuit drove with van Twiller, which may be difficult to understand, the text which he wrote and signed illustrates his sense of business:

For which aforesaid items the said Van Twiller shall pay as follows: to the West India Company for the rent remaining unpaid the sum of 500 guilders; to the aforesaid Peter Minuit the sum of one hundred and fifty guilders, to the aforesaid Company two horses, two cows, three sheep, three hogs; in return for which aforesaid items he shall be credited with the first 100 guilders which Minuit has paid on the lease and shall have the food supplies for men and animals till next harvest left there by Minuit, who was not obliged to supply them longer than the first of May 1632,[2] the said Minuit to pay the wages of the farm hands till the first of May 1632. He, Twiller, shall also have the

benefit of the increase before May 1632, that is to say, what amounts
to over and above the loss through death of the old animals; also the
improvement of the garden and newly cultivated lands as well as the
larger part of the winter seeding and all the supply of summer
seed; also the improvement of the horses during the years as also
that they are mares.

Minuit's bill of sale to van Rennselaer lacked legalistic language, and consisted of an uncomplicated transfer of livestock
for cash in florins, the amount also equal to guilders:

Two fillies born about May 1630, together	f 80
One young stallion, also born about May 1630	f 40
two milk cows three years old with calf	f 160
four heifers with calf, born 1630	f 160
two bull calves, one year old in January last	f 20
three hogs, all old sows	f 40
Total	f 500

After completing the sale of his livestock and handling
other business matters in Amsterdam, Minuit returned to his
native Rhineland where he joined his wife at Kleve. As previously pointed out, nothing was said about Gertrude Raet
Minuit in the records pertaining to New Netherland except
Wassenaer's brief note under date of November 25, 1626 that
"Minuit now sends for his wife thither." If Gertrude went to
America she must have returned to Kleve prior to his recall in
1632, although his sending for her doesn't necessarily mean
that she ever made the trip. Dr. Gorissen's research indicates
she was a property owner living in grand style in Kleve when
Minuit returned there in the spring of 1633.[3]

Minuit probably also spent time in Wesel renewing acquaintances, as well as in Emmerich. Members of his and his wife's
families were still living in these neighboring towns along the
Rhine. See Map 2. He may have attempted mercantile activities, but Germany was then torn by the Thirty Years' War
which began in 1618 and continued to disrupt the economy.
The country had become a battleground for Protestants and

Catholics, including Catholic Austria, with her Spanish allies, and Danish troops under Christian IV. At the time Minuit returned to his homeland the Swedish King Gustavus Adolphus, a champion of Protestantism, was leading 13,000 of the best trained and disciplined Swedish and Finnish troops in Europe against the German armies.

Although Protestantism was widespread among the common people in Germany, the ruling class defended Catholicism, and the religious differences led into what seemed to be endless strife. Gustavus Adolphus, known as the "Lion of the North," took German city after city and he practically mastered the country from the Elbe to the Rhine. When the news reached Kleve, Wessel, and the other Rhine towns that the Swedish monarch was killed in a victorious Swedish battle at Lützen, Minuit, like other Protestant Germans and Dutch, was saddened at the loss of a champion. They were nevertheless joyful that Protestantism was saved in Germany. Little did Minuit know that the death of King Gustavus Adolphus, a man he never saw, was to change his life in a way he could never have imagined. It began with the changing political scene in Sweden following the king's sudden death.

Gustavus Adolphus's only legitimate heir was his daughter Christina, then a child six years of age, too young to ascend to the throne. The Swedish government was placed in the hands of what was known as a regency consisting of five high noblemen in the kingdom. One of the regents, and the most influential, was the prime minister, or chancellor, Count Axel Oxenstierna, an honest, sagacious statesman. He was deeply devoted to the memory of the king he had served for 20 years and dedicated to completing unfinished tasks the king had started.

The spirit of commercial adventure had never been present in Sweden as it was in England, France, Holland, Portugal, and Spain. Gustavus Adolphus was not oblivious to the opportunities for improving Sweden's international commerce and prestige, but high-priority military matters always seemed to demand attention. Some progress had been made during his reign when a "General Trading Company," later referred to as "the Old South Company," was organized, and it encountered moderate success in minor enterprises, but eventually went out of business. After its demise, a number of investors, including the king, the Royal Council, and individual entrepreneurs in conjunction with Swedish and Finnish cities, formed in 1629-1630 what was called the "Skeppskompaniet" ("Ships' Company"). The assets and some of the vessels of the Old South Company were turned over to the new enterprise also called the United South Ship Company, but the new company did not live up to expectations and failed to exploit commerce with the New World.[4]

As a pragmatic and optimistic leader, Chancellor Oxenstierna was also realistic and he recognized that Sweden's inexperience in the international trade had to be bolstered by foreign experts who possessed know-how lacking in the kingdom. He logically turned for advice and assistance to the Netherlands whose East India and West India Companies had produced profitable trade for Dutch investors.[5] Sweden and Holland were then on friendly terms, and Sweden had representatives in Holland, and the Dutch had both diplomatic and commercial ties with Sweden. Many Dutchmen had come to Sweden to live; some served in the Swedish army; others commanded Swedish ships or worked as sailors; Swedish students went to Amsterdam to study commerce. Communication between the two countries was facilitated because the Dutch language was widely spoken in Sweden, especially among political and business leaders.

Oxenstierna's dilemma was to find Dutch executives competent to direct Swedish overseas enterprises who would come to Sweden and apply the needed expertise to meet his objectives. He was persuaded that Sweden's best opportunities lay in her copper mines which yielded immeasurable tons of copper for which there appeared to be a large potential market. The questions were where was the best place to sell the copper, and how to go about reaching the most promising customers. There were no easy answers in a day when market surveys were unknown.

Conrad von Falkenberg, a Swedish commissioner in Holland, was aware of Oxenstierna's problem, and in 1632 he wrote Oxenstierna from Holland about "an important man," one of the former directors of the West India Company, willing to assist the Swedes in forming a company to sell their copper. He said that this man did not then want his name to leak out because it might appear he had turned against his native country by divulging trade secrets to assist a foreign power. Von Falkenberg said in a letter to Oxenstierna that this man was "disgusted" with the West India Company, and would like to meet with him.[6] He added that the man proposed that the Swedes concentrate on penetrating the market in Guinea on the west coast of Africa where copper was in demand and could be exchanged for gold. Copper had ductile properties making it suitable for many practical end uses in weapons and implements, where it was impractical to use gold. Gold as a precious metal was a valuable commodity in Sweden and elsewhere in Europe and could be used to strengthen Sweden's economy.

Falkenberg had several conferences in Amsterdam in 1633 and 1634 with this mysterious man concerning the Swedish copper trade. His name was finally disclosed in confidence to Oxenstierna, and he was none other than one of Minuit's former superiors, Samuel Blommaert. He was piqued with the anti-patroon faction in the directorate of the West India Company, and like Minuit, displeased with the management of the Company's affairs in New Netherland.

There was no question that Blommaert was a well informed politico-merchant well qualified to advise the Swedish government. He was the son of an Antwerp merchant and had clerked in the houses of other merchants in Amsterdam, Hamburg, and Vienna after his father's death. At age 20 he was employed by the Dutch East India Company and was sent to the Indies. He was advanced to the position of an oppercommis (chief commercial agent) in West Borneo, and after a seven year career in the Indies returned to Holland in 1611. He became a director of the West India Company in October of 1622, serving until June 1629 when his term expired.[7] The reader has already seen that he held part ownership in several patroonships in New Netherland including Swanendael in Delaware Bay. He was reappointed a director in 1636, and at the same time he was secretly negotiating with Oxenstierna about the copper business.

Blommaert, who accumulated wealth, had private interests in copper having invested in a brass factory at Nacka southeast of Stockholm. It is not surprising that he proposed to Oxenstierna that the Crown charter a company to exploit the sale of copper on the African gold coast. Undoubtedly he had in mind investing some of his own money in the undertaking along with the Swedish backers. He had another ulterior motive — he had hopes of obtaining a permanent position as a business representative of the Swedish government in Amsterdam, as another Dutchman named Peter Spiring had obtained in the Hague.

Spiring, the son of a wealthy Dutch merchant, had adopted Sweden as his home where he found the ear of Chancellor Oxenstierna. Oxenstierna needed an official representative at the Hague who understood Dutch business methods and who could provide commercial liaison between the two governments. In 1635, Oxenstierna sent Spiring to Holland with the title of "Resident and Financial Councillor" and he became highly respected by the States General as an official representative of the Swedish Crown. He was ennobled the following year in Sweden with the title of Baron Silfverkrona which lent prestige to his position in which he was able to render valuable services to Sweden.[8] Spiring also became an intermediary between Blommaert and Oxenstierna, and many of Blommaert's letters to the chancellor went through Spiring. Since Spiring and Blommaert were countrymen, one living in Amsterdam and the other at the Hague, they frequently visited together and reached agreements on propositions to be submitted to Oxenstierna for approval. Spiring's assignment required his making trips to Sweden at regular intervals for personal consultations with the chancellor and Council of State.

Of course, Spiring participated in the discussions in both Holland and Stockholm about organizing a Swedish copper company, a project that he favored. However, before a final decision was made, Peter Minuit appeared in Amsterdam, having made a trip from Kleve in December of 1636 to discuss a new idea with Samuel Blommaert. Following Minuit's return from New Netherland he had been officially granted citizenship of Kleve on May 18, 1635, and his sympathies for the war victims in the Rhineland was a motive in generating his "new idea," although he was not yet ready for a full disclosure. In his initial interviews with Blommaert he proposed that Sweden take the initiative in getting a share of the wealth in the New World, and that he was willing to cooperate and share his experience with the Swedes.

Undoubtedly Blommaert talked to Minuit about the potential in the copper business and the possibility of Minuit accepting a position with a Swedish company directing its attention to the market in Guinea. Minuit believed that his idea would be more productive, less costly, and less risky. He maintained that there were richer commercial goals more readily attainable in the New World. Minuit stressed the opportunities for trade, and although he also had colonization in mind, he did not press that subject. Blommaert was impressed with the logic of Minuit's argument, and following their discussions he wrote a letter to Oxenstierna in which he said, "there is also another person here who has gained much experience *in another place*, and who lives in the country of Kleef; and who has, because there is a war in his country, offered his services to me and is willing to come to you and explain matters to you in person."⁹ The "place" italicized above was the New Netherland, but Blommaert was cautious about naming it because of the West India Company's activities in America.

In due course, Blommaert took Minuit to the Hague to meet Spiring who was also favorably impressed with Minuit's idea. But it was impractical to exploit the copper business in Guinea and develop the opportunities in America at the same time. Numerous discussions were held, and Blommaert and Spiring finally decided that they would recommend that the Swedes focus their attention on the New World, and this recommendation was ultimately accepted in Stockholm. It seems ironical that two Dutchmen, and a German-born son of a Walloon father should formulate plans in Holland to be executed under the aegis of the Swedish government.

The details leading up to the approval by the Swedish Council of State are covered in Blommaert's letters to Chancellor Oxenstierna. The astonishing thing is that these were unofficial letters entirely apart from diplomatic communications between the two countries. They illustrate how a private citizen of one country influenced the decisions of the head of government of another in order to achieve their common interests. Blommaert was an opportunist, and he never tried to hide the fact that he expected financial gain from investing in a Swedish enterprise, although initially he wanted this kept a secret. In one letter to the chancellor he stated frankly, "I think I might venture a lot of money in this enterprise."¹⁰ In another, he said that he preferred to invest his money in Minuit's name "for several reasons, one of which is that I am still in the service of the West India Company. I will probably resign after my return from my visit to you [he hoped Oxenstierna would hire him]; I would not like to have my reputation damaged."¹¹ Obviously, if Blommaert could announce to his Dutch colleagues that Sweden had initiated an offer that he could not reject, he would have a valid reason for explaining his collaboration. Until such an association could be concluded he felt that it was to his best advantage not to reveal that he was investing money in the interests of a rival country.

Through the exchange of correspondence, and Spiring's trips to Sweden, agreement was reached that Swedish investors, including the chancellor himself, would contribute 50% to the American enterprise, and Dutch investors, including Blommaert, would also contribute 50%. Early in the discussions in Holland between Blommaert and Spiring it was decided that Minuit would accompany Spiring on one of his scheduled trips to Sweden to be presented to the chancellor. Minuit would then make a presentation to the Swedish leaders and explain his proposal in detail. Minuit doubtless looked forward with excitement and anticipation to his first trip to Sweden, but something occurred causing him to defer the trip.

Personal matters in Emmerich caused Minuit to return to the Rhineland from Holland, although the reasons were not recorded. As a consequence Spiring made the trip alone to see the chancellor, taking with him a letter Minuit had written outlining his proposal.

This letter was dated June 15, 1636, and apparently Minuit intended it to be read by Spiring and then delivered to Oxenstierna, or the substance read to him. It is significant as a "conception memorandum" in which Minuit envisioned a colony in America which he called New Sweden, and explained what would be needed and how much it would cost. Because of its historical importance the letter is fully quoted below in an English translation of the original Dutch. Of particular note is that Minuit voluntarily offered his services to Sweden; he said he would make a settlement in places well known to him; he stated that by obtaining furs from the Indians, especially beaver pelts, and raising tobacco and grains, that the project would be profitable to Sweden; he recommended that a trading company be

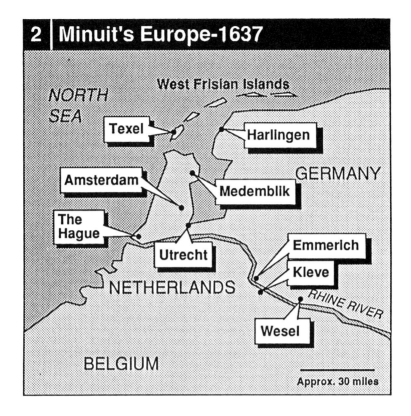

2 | Minuit's Europe-1637

NORTH SEA

West Frisian Islands

Texel

Harlingen

Amsterdam

Medemblik

GERMANY

The Hague

Utrecht

Emmerich

Kleve

NETHERLANDS

RHINE RIVER

Wesel

BELGIUM

Approx. 30 miles

chartered by the Swedish government to trade exclusively in the New World for 20 years with a 10 year exemption from paying import duties on all shipments made from America to Sweden. In short, he proposed the formation of a commercial organization patterned after the Dutch West India Company with whose operations he was thoroughly familiar. He deliberately made no reference to those of his countrymen who had lost their homes and farms during the war because that was something that was ·of concern to him but not to the Swedish Crown. The letter reads as follows:[12]

> As navigation makes kingdoms and countries thrive and in the West-Indies many places gradually come to be occupied by the English, Dutch, and French, I think the Swedish Crown ought not to stand back and refrain from having her name spread widely, also in

foreign countries; and to that end I the undersigned, wish to offer my services to the Swedish Crown to set out modestly on what might, by God's grace, become something great within a short period of time.

Firstly, I have suggested to Mr. Pieter Spiering to make a journey to the Virginias, New Netherland and other places, in which regions certain places are well known to me, with a very good climate, which could be named *Nova Sweediae* [New Sweden].

For the equipment of such an expedition would be needed a ship of 60-70-100 lasts, fitted with 17 guns and proportional ammunition.

For the cargo, consisting of adzes, axes, kettles, duffelcoats and other merchandise, 10,000 to 12,000 guilders would be needed.

For equipment for a crew of 20 to 25 men, and provisions for 12 months, about 3,400 guilders would be needed.

In case the Swedish Crown is willing to provide the ship and ammunition, together with 12 soldiers to take the places into possession and hold them, and also a small bark or yacht to sail around with and trade, the total equipment would cost about 16,000 guilders, half of which I offer to pay myself, and Mr. Spiering will pay the other half later, in cash, either on his own account or on behalf of the Swedish Crown.

The best time to set sail would be the sooner the better; although trade only starts in spring it is better to be there early, so that we can make friends with the savages in order to have them collect many furs during the winter; and we might trade 4, 5, or 6,000 beaver-skins, and setting out in this small way we can enlarge our capital and start on more substantial projects later.

The Swedish Crown should grant the beginners of this new voyage a charter, prohibiting any one to sail from Sweden to the area from Terra Neuf [Newfoundland] to Florida for the next 20 years, on the penalty of confiscation of ship and cargo; and they should also be granted to attack Spanish and Portuguese ships, which are often carried over at sea, and take them to Sweden as good [lawful] prizes.

Also, all imported and exported goods of the Company should be duty-free for the next 10 years.

And as this country is suitable for growing tobacco and all sorts of grains, it would be wise to take along some competent people who could at the same time be of use as keepers of the furs.

In addition, it could be indicated orally what advantages the Swedish Crown might gain in due time; I could either be summoned to Sweden to give further explanation, or else the gentlemen of the Government can act as they see fit.

This is, in short, to serve Your Honour as a memorandum. Your Honour is asked to send answer from Sweden to the known friend whether the plan is to be carried out, in order not to lose time and keep others from occupying what would be of great use to the Crown of Sweden. Hereby wishing you luck on your journey, I remain,

Your Excellency's faithful servant,

Amsterdam, June 15, 1636   Pieter Minuit

Minuit's offer to pay one-half of the cost of the "total equipment," or 8,000 guilders, should not be taken literally. It is extremely unlikely that he had that much cash to invest. Blommaert had assured him that he would be able to raise half of the cost of the expedition if the Swedes through Spiring acting as their surrogate would put up a like sum. Blommaert still did not want his name disclosed to the West India Company since he was still angling with Oxenstierna to get on the Swedish payroll. Spiring, Oxenstierna, and Minuit all knew that Blommaert could raise the amount needed, but Minuit did not know whose eyes would see his letter. Thus, he was guarded in his use of Blommaert's name which is why in the final paragraph of the letter he refers to "the known friend." Both Spiring and Oxenstierna knew that he meant Blommaert.

Minuit's proposed plan was a complete reversal of the one under consideration for developing the copper business. Instead of exporting an indigenous Swedish product to foreign customers at the risks in developing a new market, he proposed forming a company to import products from America, i.e., furs, tobacco, and grains, to sell in a market already existing in Sweden and other European countries.

Spiring had a meeting with the Swedish Council of State on September 27, 1636, and after completing his business in Sweden he returned to the Hague arriving November 8. He had good news to pass on to Blommaert. First, the Swedes favored Minuit's proposal, and Oxenstierna wanted Minuit to come to Stockholm to consult with him without delay and lay plans for the expedition to America. Secondly, Spiring had been authorized by the chancellor and Council of State to employ Blommaert as an agent working for the Swedish Crown in Holland, a sort of consul general. He was to be paid a yearly salary of 1,000 R.D. plus certain per diem travel expense. This would give Blommaert a valid reason for resigning from the directorate of the Dutch West India Company, although he continued to withhold information from the other directors that Sweden was planning an expedition to America. He was aware that "certain places well known to me" to which Minuit referred in his letter meant territory which the Dutch would claim was part of the New Netherland. Nothing could be gained by upsetting the directors and provoking questions in the States General which might block the Swedish initiative.

Blommaert dispatched a letter to Minuit giving him the good news and requesting him to return to Holland promptly.[13] Minuit had evidently taken over the supervision of his wife's inherited property at Kleve where the inhabitants had not yet recovered from a devastating Spanish attack on July 27 and 28, 1635 which ruined cities, villages, and farms. A discussion of this warfare and the land ravaged by enemy troops would necessitate digressing from our main story, but its relevancy to Minuit's life lies in the decisions that had to be made to the property in his custody. His wife's brother, Goert Raet, who had been elected mayor of Kleve for three consecutive years, 1626 to 1629, and his immediate family, also were property owners. The writer does not know whether Goert Raet was still living, or whether other male members of the family could look after his wife's interests, but Minuit must have made provisions for her care.

He could not suppress his energy and adventurous spirit, nor the magnetism that attracts an entrepreneur to a new commercial challenge. He did what was needed to be done and made ready for a trip to Holland with the expectation of going to Stockholm from there. Time was of the essence because Blommaert, Spiring, and Oxenstierna were demanding immediate action. Minuit himself had urged "the sooner the better" in his June 15 letter in order to be in America in time to trade with the Indians in the spring of 1638.

Moreover, the Spanish attack on Kleve emphasized to him the urgency to take action on the plan he had in mind to assist his countrymen. He had brought this up with Blommaert, not as one of the objectives of the first expedition, but as the aim of later voyages. Possibly he and Blommaert agreed that it was not timely to discuss this subject with the Swedes, and it was not brought out during the preparations for the first voyage. A year later it was revealed in one of Blommaert's letters in which he wrote:

> Since Peter Minuit lived in the land of Kleef, which land and the neighboring countries, too, is spoiled by war and poverty, it was his plan to get some people from there and give them a free voyage, together with some cattle, and give them some rights in the new country, as some founders of New Netherland have done.[14]

This scheme of Minuit's looms as a personal objective in his determination to lay the foundations for a permanent colony. Apparently he believed that assisting farmers in the Rhineland impoverished by the war to find new homes in New Sweden should wait for the next expedition. Priority had to be given to making a foothold in America before it was timely to talk specifically to the Swedes about absorbing the cost of transporting German settlers and their families.

While Minuit was preparing for his trip to Holland and Stockholm, Spiring and Blommaert were working on the details of forming a company "that is to sail to the East American shores between Terra Nova [Newfoundland] and Florida to trade there." This was the identical area which Minuit mentioned for Swedish exploitation in his letter of June 15. No specific site within this area was named, but Minuit knew exactly where he would make the first settlement, but Spiring and Blommaert agreed with Minuit that it was wiser to talk in general terms to avoid antagonizing the West India Company if the news leaked out. In their plans for the new company the two Dutchmen stressed trade because it would immediately yield a cash return. Neither had any compelling interest in investing money to transplant Swedish culture to the New World or of assisting hungry families in the Rhineland.

When Minuit arrived in Holland in December, Blommaert and Spiring immediately engaged him in a series of conferences because much unfinished business awaited his advice and endorsement. Only he could be specific about a land with which he was thoroughly familiar and what was needed to get established there without affronting the Dutch West India Company. Minuit made clear that a direct confrontation should be avoided, and that no settlement should be made on land where the Company had a trading post or could produce deeds showing they had bought the land from the Indians.

No one knew better than Minuit that Dutch ships had been going in and out of Delaware Bay and River (where he intended to settle) for many years as far back as 1616, and that the patroons had made a settlement at Swanendael although the men placed there were all massacred by the Indians. He knew the Dutch considered the Delaware River valley as part of New Netherland, but the bounds were inexact. Furthermore, as of 1636 there was no Dutch settlement or trading post on the western bank of the Delaware River, although Fort Nassau built at present Gloucester on the east bank of the river during his administration was still in use. He considered the west bank of the Delaware as being adjacent to New Netherland, but not part of it. A Swedish settlement there should not run afoul of Dutch interests especially if he could persuade the Indians to deed the land to the Swedes.

All of this had to be explained to the Swedish Council of State, and their many questions answered before assent was given in Stockholm to launch the expedition. Minuit took with him to Sweden the following 16 separate documents jointly prepared by Blommaert, Spiring, and himself intended to answer all the questions that would be raised:[15]

1. Conditions upon which the company shall be formed
2. Draft of the conditions: What the very laudable government of Sweden shall be pleased to do for the company
3. Instructions to serve Peter Minuit on the voyage[16]
4. Instructions for the marine council on the voyage
5. Ration list
6. Plan for distributing food
7. List of wet and dry foodstuffs for 36 men for 15 months
8. Memorandum of how the commissaries and other officials shall prepare their reports
9. List of munitions
10. Instructions for Peter Minuit on his voyage to Sweden
11. Mariner's chart of the entire West Indies and Florida
12. Tally of all the casks that are needed aboard ship for a long voyage
13. Salt license that is to be given to chartered ships for transshipment[17]
14. Regulations
15. Extract from commissaries' instructions
16. Bill of lading form

    2 parcels of letters for His Excellency the Chancellor
These contain Mr. Spierinck's letters to his Excellency
and to Her Majesty.
    1 parcel with all the papers mentioned above.
    1 parcel of letters to Admiral Fleming, containing two
letters from me [Blommaert] and one
from Spierinck.

Admiral Fleming to whom Minuit was supposed to deliver certain letters was Klas Larsson Fleming, who was born in Louhisaari, Finland in 1592. Son of a prominent Finnish noble, he received the education and training customary among Finnish and Swedish aristocracy, after which he embarked on a military career. He rose rapidly, and in 1620 was appointed vice-admiral of the Swedish fleet, and in 1629 became chief of the naval forces in the kingdom. After King Gustavus Adolphus's death he became a member of the regency running the country. When the national Board of Trade (also known as the Commercial College) was established in 1637 to increase and extend foreign commerce, he became its president.[18] Blommaert and Spring were convinced that if Fleming's interest could be aroused he would play a decisive part in assuring the success of the American project.

Not the least important of the above documents was No. 11, the mariner's chart showing all of the West Indies and the "Florida coast" which did not mean the present state of Florida, but extensive territory along the Atlantic seaboard. This was probably a manuscript map copied from one owned by the West India Company. As company executives, Blommaert and Minuit both had access to maps which illustrated geographical features not yet shown on engraved maps. Maps of New World waters and the New Netherland territory were then extremely rare in Sweden which is why Blommaert wanted Minuit to show the latest ones in confidence to Oxenstierna. Because of international rivalries there was then no free exchange between nations of cartographical data. This was one of many assets that Minuit could share with the Swedes, and Blommaert believed that Oxenstierna would be impressed with Minuit's presentations because he intimately knew the territory and the waterways. Minuit left Holland on February 1 for his first trip to the Swedish capital.

On February 18, 1637, Blommaert wrote Oxenstierna that he had received a letter from Minuit written in Hamburg and he expected to be in Stockholm by the end of the month.[19] Hamburg on the Elbe River was an important trading center and transfer point having regular postal service with Sweden. See Map 3. Minuit could have gone there overland from Kleve or on a packet vessel from Holland to connect with a vessel to Sweden. Spiring may have asked him to confer with a Hamburg resident named Joachim Stumpff who had proposed to Oxenstierna that Sweden become active in the West India Trade.[20] If so, no record has been preserved of their conversation, but nothing came of Stumpff's proposal.

Minuit pressed on to Stockholm from Hamburg arriving in the middle of March, delayed because he became ill on the trip, and his condition worsened by the time he reached his destination. The nature of his illness was not identified, but undiagnosed fevers and contagious intestinal ailments were prevalent in Germany during the war years. Despite his weakened condition he laid the proposed plans before Admiral Fleming and the Council of State in a very convincing presentation. No doubt he also had a private audience with Oxenstierna to answer the chancellor's questions. There is no indication that Minuit was presented to the little princess Christina who would grow up to become an erratic queen, but at her tender years she would not have understood what was afoot.

The result of the conferences was that the Swedish leaders reached an agreement to form the New Sweden Company which would sponsor an expedition under Minuit's direction. In the political-commercial system of the day, government officials were permitted to invest in a company along with private investors. The government could also make contributions in money, goods, or the loan of ships to the company. In these interlocking ties, officials of the government could also become officers in a private company. This concept was unlike that in the modern American business world where private enterprise is separate from the legislative and executive branches of the government, although federal statutes may exercise restraints on how a company operates its business. In the case of the New Sweden Company, the Crown, from the time of its formation, took a strong position in all the details of its operation.

For example, the government decided that instead of one ship and a sloop, which Minuit originally proposed, that the expedition should consist of two vessels large enough to cross the Atlantic — a ship and a yacht. These vessels would be made available by the admiralty. A smaller sloop would be constructed in Sweden, but disassembled before the vessels sailed, and the component parts carried aboard the ship. When the two vessels reached their destination, the ships' carpenters would reassemble the sloop and it would remain in New Sweden for use in the Indian trade. It was to be built small enough to navigate inland waters, as well as the larger rivers, but it was not designed for ocean travel. The addition of the yacht meant an increase in Minuit's projected cost estimates, but he did not oppose it because it would strengthen the project. Furthermore, Admiral Fleming became enthusiastic about the expedition after hearing Minuit's presentation, and favored a second vessel. Fleming's endorsement guaranteed the support of the admiralty, as well as the new Board of Trade over which he presided.

The welcome news was transmitted to Blommaert and Spiring in Holland through the slow process of sailing vessels carrying the mails, or by personal messengers. Blommaert was authorized to purchase the needed supplies and to hire sailors in Holland because of the shortage in Sweden of experienced seamen. Admiral Fleming was no novice in outfitting naval vessels, but the Swedes believed that this task could be better handled by Blommaert and Minuit in Holland. They knew exactly what kind of supplies would be needed on the expedition, and Blommaert had contact with Dutch producers on whom he could place orders. He and Minuit knew what qualifications were expected of crews sailing in waters unfamiliar to the Swedes. Blommaert expected Minuit to return to Holland to participate with him in the preparations for the voyage.

Admiral Fleming agreed to recommend the selection of two vessels, have them rigged, and ready at Gothenburg, which had been selected as the port of embarkation. The sailors hired in Holland would report for duty at Gothenburg, and the merchandise purchased in Holland would be shipped in care of the customs collector there. When everything converged at the Gothenburg port, the ships could be made ready for the long voyage. See Map 3 on page 105.

To avoid losing time, Blommaert advanced the funds needed to purchase supplies in Holland pending approval of the financial details in Stockholm and the receipt of cash from Swedish investors. The Swedes were responsible for calculating the total amount of cash needed, and each subscriber consented to furnish part of the sum which in the aggregate would total 50% of the cost. Profit and losses would be shared equally by Dutch and Swedish investors on a per capita basis proportionate to their individual investments.

On May 16, 1637, Blommaert wrote to Oxenstierna that "Fleming sent me a draft of the company and who are to participate in it on the Swedish side, and he asks me to do the same here; this will happen as soon as Minuit arrives who himself will participate for one-eighth."[21]

Blommaert does not specifically refer to a charter issued by the Swedish Crown although the earlier companies had been officially chartered. No charter for the New Sweden Company has been preserved, although a leading historian believes that one was executed, but no longer exists. Another historian is of the opinion that no charter was granted the company.[22] After reading the Blommaert-Oxenstierna correspondence, the writer finds it difficult to believe that Blommaert could have raised funds among sophisticated Dutch businessmen unless the Swedish government had spelled out in a document the privileges it had granted the company and how long those privileges would apply, especially the exclusive right to trade in America, and non-payment of import duties.

The Swedes were slow in raising their share of the money which irritated Blommaert, who was eager to get the expedition on the way before winter set in, and everything he bought had to be paid for in cash. Without going into details, this was finally resolved. Then a more serious crisis delayed the project. Minuit's health continued to decline. He became bedfast in Stockholm, and his illness seemed critical.

Unaware of the seriousness of Minuit's illness, Blommaert impatiently awaited his arrival in Amsterdam. He wrote Oxenstierna to report he had shipped some supplies to Gothenburg, but added, "If only Minuit were here now, so that I could talk with him about the expedition and then go to Sweden to inform you and the government about the expedition in person."[23]

When the mail from Sweden brought Blommaert the disturbing news about Minuit's illness, he wrote, "I hope that God gives him good health since we would lose much time if we were to find another suitable person."[24] This was an understatement — who could have replaced Minuit? Someone else might have been found because Blommaert knew that no man is indispensable, but it would have been impossible to find a substitute having Minuit's unique experience and qualifications to lead the expedition. Certainly there was no one in Sweden equal to the assignment, and the Swedes knew it too.

In May of 1637, Minuit was still on a sick bed in Stockholm, more than two months after his arrival in Sweden. He was lodged in the residence or inn of one Frans Weinschenck, and Admiral Fleming was paying his bills for lodging, doctor, and medicine.[25] One can only draw the conclusion that Minuit had exhausted his cash. The Swedes were evidently optimistic about his recovery for capital was secured for the enterprise during his illness, but the records make no further reference to his subscribing to one-eighth share. When the books were closed for the initial voyage, the subscribers were as follows:[26]

Swedish

Chancellor Axel Oxenstierna ⅛ part   1800 R.D. [Riksdaler]
Gabriel Gustaffson Oxenstierna ⅛ part 1800 R.D.
   [the chancellor's brother, the state "bailiff"]
Admiral Klas Fleming ¹⁄₁₆ part   900 R.D.
Gabriel Bengtsson Oxenstierna ¹⁄₁₆ part   900 R.D.
   [Chancellor of the Exchequer]
Peter Spiring ⅛ part   <u>1800 R.D.</u>
        Total   7200 R.D.

Dutch

Adam Bessels $\frac{1}{16}$ part	900 R.D.
Isaac von dem Waeter $\frac{3}{14}$ part	675 R.D.
Gillies von Brugge $\frac{1}{64}$ part	225 R.D.
Jaris Hoeffnaegell $\frac{1}{16}$ part	900 R.D.
Huygens von Arnheim $\frac{1}{16}$ part	900 R.D.
Samuel Blommaert $\frac{1}{4}$ part	3600 R.D.
Total	7200 R.D.

The total capitalization of 14,400 riksdaler (each equal to 2½ guilders) was a substantial amount of money, equivalent to the buying power of many thousands of American dollars. To get a grasp of its magnitude perhaps it might be compared to raising between $500,000 and $750,000 for a project today. Samuel Blommaert was the largest investor having subscribed twice the amount pledged by the Swedish chancellor! It is conceivable that his part may have included ⅛ which he extended on credit to Minuit, but this is a supposition without documentation.

The money to cover the expenses of the voyage had been raised; Admiral Fleming requested Blommaert to hire 25 or 30 men "experienced at sea," and Spiring cleared the request with the Dutch States General who consented to Blommaert hiring sailors and officers in Amsterdam.[27]

Blommaert did not reveal either to the sailors he hired or the States General that a Swedish expedition was being prepared to sail to America. None of his activities aroused undue curiosity in Holland because he had long been engaged in the mercantile business. Transporting sailors and supplies to Gothenburg did not cause any stir because 50% of the vessels entering the Baltic were flying Dutch colors and transporting a wide range of products. It was also common practice for Dutch sailors and sea captains to report to Gothenburg for assignments on vessels whose destinations were not publicized.

Blommaert ordered additional supplies for the vessels, and trade goods to be used in bartering with the Indians, including cloth woven on special order in Kampen and Leyden. As early as May 1637, 2,748 ½ yards of cloth and several hogsheads of distilled liquors were shipped to Sweden in care of the customs collector at Gothenburg with additional shipments to follow. Admiral Fleming was making plans to have two vessels sail from Stockholm to Gothenburg where they would pick up the Dutch sailors and take the cargo aboard. But the expedition still did not have a commander. Would it have to be delayed further, or possibly cancelled, at a loss to the investors, because of the gravity of Minuit's illness?

Chapter 4 Notes

1. *VRBM*, pp. 223-24.
2. May 1, 1632 appears to have been the official date when Minuit's financial obligations to the Company were terminated.
3. Friedrich Gorissen, "Peter Minuit und die Stadt Kleve," *Kalendar fur das Klever Land*," Boss-Druck und Verlag, Kleve, 1982, p. 114. After Minuit's death, Gertrude, who was financially secure, occupied a large house in Kleve where she was living in 1653. The date of her death is unknown, *ibid.*, p. 115.
4. This early history is fully covered in *SS* 1.
5. See *SS* 1, Chapter 11 for background.
6. *Ibid.*, p. 88.
7. Biographical notes in *Pelts and Palisades*, pp. 161-64.
8. *SS* 2:695-96.
9. *Blommaert Letters*, No. 9, Dec. 26, 1635. These letters, numbered by Kernkamp, have never been translated into English. Translations of the relevant passages relating to Minuit were made for the author by W.A. Hoffstädt and F.W.H. Hoffstädt of Zwolle, the Netherlands. Quotations

appearing in the text are from their translations which
have been deposited in the Kalmar Nyckel Foundation
along with photocopies of the Kernkamp 1908 publication, and photocopies of the original manuscript letters
kindly made available by the Royal Archives in Sweden
through the courtesy of Mr. and Mrs. Allen C. Rawl.

10. Letter No. 20, Feb. 11, 1637.
11. Letter No. 24, May 16, 1637.
12. An English translation of the letter by Gregory B. Keen
    was published in the *Pennsylvania Magazine of History
    and Biography* 6:458-60, 1881, and reprinted in Keen's
    essay "New Sweden, or the Swedes on the Delaware" in
    Narratives and Critical History of America, ed. Justin
    Windsor (Riverside Press, Cambridge, 1884), pp. 445-6,
    n. The above is a new English translation made by
    W.A. Hoffstädt and F.W.H. Hoffstädt.
13. Letter No. 19, Jan. 14, 1637. For Blommaert's appoint-
    ment, see *SS* 1:99.
14. Letter No. 35, Nov. 13, 1638.
15. Letter No. 20, Feb. 11, 1637. Dr. Charles Gehring kindly
    made the English translation of the list for the author.
16. An English translation by the late Dr. A.R. Dunlap of
    these instructions written in Dutch may be found in
    Weslager, 1961, pp. 168-81. Some alterations were made
    in Sweden in the copy Minuit carried with him.
17. The Instructions, *ibid.*, p. 178 charge Minuit to ascertain
    if salt could be obtained in the West Indies. In the event
    that he brought back salt with him, it was necessary for
    him to fill out a certificate so it could be imported without
    paying a duty. Salt was scarce in Sweden and was often
    obtained in Spain and Portugal; it was principally used
    as a preservative for meat and fish.
18. John E. Wuorinen, *The Finns on the Delaware*, (New
    York: Columbia University Press, 1938), pp. 39-40.
19. Letter No. 20, Feb. 11, 1637. He also wrote Blommaert

from Helsingör, Denmark on Feb. 22, *SS* 1:105, n. 2.
20. *SS* 1:100-101.
21. Letter No. 24, May 16, 1637.
22. *SS* 1:107; Stellan Dahlgren and Hans Norman, *The Rise and Fall of New Sweden* (Stockholm: Almqvist & Wiksell, 1988), p. 4.
23. Letter No. 25, June 6, 1637.
24. Letter No. 24, May 16, 1637.
25. *SS* 1:105 n.
26. *Ibid.*, p. 106.
27. *Ibid.*, pp. 109-10.

5. Preparations For The Voyage

Peter Minuit's recovery from his illness came slowly. Swedish physicians doubtless puzzled over his symptoms, and prescribing for a strange illness continued to be a matter of trial and error. Once Minuit reached a turning point, his restlessness to get out of the sick bed convinced Admiral Fleming that his energy was returning and the expedition would soon become a reality. The other investors in the New Sweden Company, both Dutch and Swedish, who were concerned about the amount Blommaert was spending to support the expedition, also felt relieved. The Swedish officeholders in the company were less aware of the high cost of doing business in America than were Dutch investors who had a better understanding of overseas commerce. On the other hand, their motivation was a quick return on their money and they were less tolerant of delays.

The names of the officials in the New Sweden Company are not known because the charter for the company has not yet been found, if one existed. Fleming may have had the title of president or director, but this is still unproven. From what has been recorded about the company, there is no question that he became a driving force in promoting the New Sweden project. His office as president of the Board of Trade gave added weight to his participation and recommendations.[1]

Toward the end of July 1637, while Minuit was still convalescing in Stockholm, Blommaert hired experienced sailors in Holland, advanced some of their wages, and paid for their voyage to Gothenburg. At the same time people on his staff were scouting for sources of supply for the cargo, and supplies needed by the crew. Minuit had written him that barrels were then scarce in Sweden, and Blommaert lost no time in having a number made in various sizes, strengthened with iron hoops, which he also shipped to Gothenburg. Since the base of the expedition was hundreds of miles from the source of most of the supplies, the goods had to be loaded in Amsterdam, unloaded in Gothenburg, and loaded again on the ships. It is a credit to Blommaert's diligent planning and scheduling that everything worked out as well as it did.

The Swedish admiralty was slow in selecting ships from the fleet at Stockhom to take the expedition to America from Gothenburg. Fleming became impatient with the navy's inaction, and as a result of his demands, the government issued an order on June 30 to the admirals "to prepare two ships and man them with thirty-six boatsmen."[2] Some time elapsed for these orders to clear through organization channels, and the two ships did not leave their anchorage at the Skeppsholm in Stockholm until the middle of August with Captain Anders Nilsson Krober in command of one, and Lieutenant Jacob Barber of the other. They apparently understood they would be replaced by new officers in Gothenburg. It was a 10-day voyage south on the Baltic to Oland which lies opposite Kalmar, thence to Malmö and north through the Öresund which separates Denmark from Sweden, and into the Skattegat. See Map 3.

In the meantime, Minuit was on his feet again making ready for his return to Amsterdam. He knew that Blommaert was

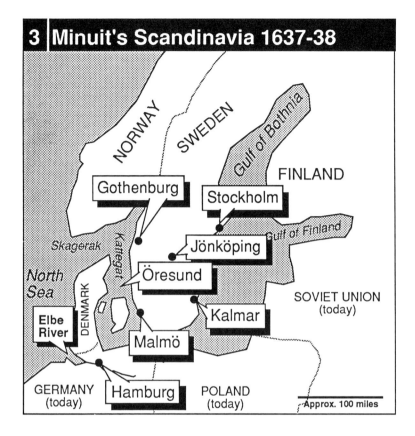

Map labels: NORWAY, SWEDEN, Gulf of Bothnia, FINLAND, Gothenburg, Stockholm, Gulf of Finland, Skagerak, Kattegat, Jönköping, North Sea, Öresund, DENMARK, SOVIET UNION (today), Elbe River, Kalmar, Malmö, GERMANY (today), Hamburg, POLAND (today), Approx. 100 miles

waiting to consult with him about the expedition and to approve the selection of officers to fill the remaining openings. When he left Sweden in early August he must have still been very weak, and perhaps he was able to rest on the voyage through the Skagerak and the North Sea to Texel at the mouth of the Zuyder Zee, Amsterdam's nearest seaport. The weather in those waters was unusually pleasant in July and August in contrast to winter storms which came later.

There was little time for rest when he reached Amsterdam. Among many things that remained to be done, Blommaert had two barber-surgeons for him to interview. It was important to select competent men, because the welfare of the personnel depended upon these "doctors" who treated ailments, performed surgery, pulled teeth, cured serious ills by bleeding the patients, and also cut hair and trimmed beards. After the barber-surgeons were signed up, Blommaert wrote that "as navigating officer we enlisted Michiel Symonsz, a fine and honest man who has sailed the coast of Florida for many years, and who will take over leadership in case Minuit dies."[3]

On August 22, Blommaert wrote Oxenstierna, "I sent nearly all the goods to Götenburg this week. The rest will go with Minuit, two barbers and other officers, in the hope that the ships will be in Götenburg soon to set out on the expedition. For several reasons I wish they could have left a month earlier, for it is now late in the year to go around England, which must be done, however, to avoid the Dunkirk pirates."[4]

This seems to mean that the preferred route was through the English channel, and from there to the Azores or the Canary Islands, but vessels from Sweden were forced to take a longer route around the British Isles to avoid attack by pirates in the narrow Straits of Dover. With winter approaching the weather was less favorable for sailing around England and Scotland than it would have been if the vessels had departed earlier.

Blommaert continued to complain in his letters about the slowness of the Swedes in compensating him for cash he had spent, and that the Swedish Council of State was responsible for the added expense of outfitting and supplying a yacht which was not included in Minuit's original proposal. But, he added in one letter, "a rich Spanish ship will make up for it." In another he refers to the possibility of the yacht capturing some "good fish," namely Spanish prizes. Not only was gold and silver worth seizing, "but a rich Spanish prize with 300-400 boxes of sugar will make up for the [excess] costs."[5] The possibility of raiding Spanish vessels had been openly discussed in the Council of State and it was a very real objective. The Swedes considered it a lawful pursuit just as the Dutch West India Company did.

The records tell nothing about whether or not Minuit went to Kleve to see his wife while he was in Amsterdam — it had been eight or nine months since they last saw each other. Knowing that he was about to embark for Sweden and from thence to America, he may have wanted to say goodbye to her. But this is not known, nor is there a record of the date of his return to Sweden except that he was back in Gothenburg early in September of 1637 making plans for embarkation. What a dramatic scene it would have been if he had sailed into the Gothenburg port at the same time the two vessels selected for the voyage — the *Kalmar Nyckel* and the *Fogel Grip* — arrived from Stockholm. The date of their arrival is not known either.

The *Kalmar Nyckel*, which means "Key of Kalmar," was named for a fortress that protected the city of Kalmar; it was the key, so to speak, in protecting the city. *Fogel Grip*, meaning "Bird Griffin" was the name of a mythical four-legged creature having the body and tail of a lion and the head and wings of an eagle. Griffin was a popular name for ships in Sweden and there is record of a *Stora Gripen (The Large Griffin)* and a *Lilla Gripen (The Small Griffin).*[6] These names were often abbreviated to *Grip* or *Gripen*; the *en* in Swedish is the article *the*. Because of the duplication of the name, it was possible for one *Grip* to be confused with another. The *Fogel Grip* is not particularized in the records with a description other than it was an armed vessel owned by the South Company, loaned to the navy, and termed a jaght, (yacht). This term, which originated with the Dutch, had nothing to do with pleasure boating, but it meant a swift craft or hunter. The Dutch also used the word bojort for similar sturdy craft. Although smaller than the *Kalmar Nyckel*, the *Grip* was fast and maneuverable, and Minuit immediately recognized she would be useful in hunting down Spanish prey in the Caribbean.

Minuit was much more impressed with the *Kalmar Nyckel*. She was neat and trim silhouetted in the harbor against the blue Swedish sky, the gilded lion on her figurehead, and the blue flag of Sweden with its gold cross streaming from her mainmast. She had been refurbished from stem to stern with her gunwales and forecastle painted an indigo blue. As he saw her it was natural that he would be reminded of the *New Netherland*, launched six years before at Manhattan during his administration. He had been proud of the *New Netherland*, but never had the opportunity to command her, or any other vessel for that matter. He saw the *Kalmar Nyckel* as a smaller version of the *New Netherland*, and his thoughts may have flashed back to his boyhood on the Rhine where he had first been exposed to sailing vessels carrying grain and other farm products to Utrecht and Rotterdam. In his career Minuit had known many Dutch vessels including *Den Orangeboom (The Orange Tree)* which brought him on his first voyage to New Netherland, the *Meeuwken (Little Seamew)* on his second trip, and the *Eendracht (Unity)* which took him back to England as he ended his career with the West India Company. Now he had the opportunity not only to supervise a vessel, but to command an expedition to the New World.

What made the *Kalmar Nyckel* seem distinctly Dutch to him was her poop, a superstructure built to house the captain's cabin, its roof constituting an elevated deck where the commander standing with legs spread, his back to the wind, could survey the entire vessel as her prow cleaved the sea. From this raised deck he could watch the square sails taking to the main and foretop masts like giant swans unfolding their wings as calloused hands steadied the ropes to keep her from soaring away. There was no doubt about it — she was to be his ship, and it was love at first sight.

Minuit did not then know how the *Kalmar Nyckel* had found her way into the Swedish navy, but it did not take long for him to learn her story which dated back to the days when Gustavus Adolphus was still on the Swedish throne. In 1629 the king decided to increase the Swedish navy and the merchant marine, but capital was hard to raise due to other demands on the state treasury. He called a meeting early in the year of representatives from various towns and cities in the kingdom and proposed founding the Skeppskompaniet (Ships company) referred to in the previous chapter. The proposal was favorably received, and it was decided that 16 ships 100 to 150 feet long, armed with 12 to 16 cannon each, were to be furnished; Stockholm was to prepare four, Gothenburg two, and the smaller cities, arranged in groups, to pool their money and provide the remaining ten.

The ships were to be used for commercial voyages, either by the cities themselves, or by the Crown at a rate based on the freight income, to be paid the cities. In the event of war the ships would be used to protect the country against the enemy. The intent was to build the ships in Sweden to stimulate industry, but since time was limited, a number of cities requested and were given approval to hire or buy vessels abroad.

Complications due to limited finances, and other reasons, caused delays in executing the plans, although these details are not of immediate concern to our story. The relevant facts are that the cities of Kalmar and Jönköping acting together assumed the responsibilities of ac'uiring a ship. Two agents, Olof Persson and Måns Jonsson, the 'atter representing Kalmar, prepared to go to Holland for the pu'oose of buying a ship with money raised by the Skeppskompan.'ets Kalmargrupp (the Ship Company's Kalmar Group). A Swedish writer reports what then may have occurred:

> Kalmar had in April [of 1629] sent two representatives to Holland. When they arrived in the Öresund they found there a counter-ship, a pinnace of 130 lasts. With this, one of the representatives went to Holland to buy the ship. The author is inclined to suppose that this ship was the later well-known *Kalmar Nyckel*.[7]

The key word in the above quotation translated as "counter ship" is "spegelskepp," a specific term for a ship built with what was known as an "akter spegel," namely a square stern.[8]

The high stern or poop of the *Kalmar Nyckel* meets this description. She was one of a class of Dutch armed merchant ships known as a "pinasschip" which the Swedes called a pinass, or pinnace. The Dutch and Scandinavian meanings of the term differed from the English pinnace which was a tender or a smaller boat. When she was built in Holland, sometime prior to April 1629, she presumably had a Dutch name, but like an adopted baby, her purchasers gave her a new Swedish name, *Kalmar Nyckel*, to bring her into the Swedish naval family. The identity of the shipyard in the Netherlands where she was built has eluded researchers.

A sum of 13,450 silver daler has been given as the price the Kalmargrupp paid the Dutch for the vessel, although the writer has not been able to authenticate this figure.[9] At the time of her purchase she is said to have been armed with 14 six pound cast iron cannon and two six pound "metal guns," which presumably meant copper.[10] In his letter of June 15, 1636 (see preceding chapter) Minuit stated that a vessel carrying 17 guns would be needed, but this was a preliminary estimate. Undoubtedly the armament on the *Kalmar Nyckel* varied from time to time, and the number of cannon she carried, which were moveable on their wheels, depended upon the nature of the missions.

In 1634 the government took over the *Kalmar Nyckel*, and although she may have served now and then as a merchant vessel, her main use seems to have been as a warship. In 1648 she is shown on a list of the admiralty ships as carrying 40 sailors, 28 soldiers, and 12 cannon which may have been her wartime strength.[11] The records of the New Sweden Company do not refer to the number of cannon she carried on her maiden American voyage, but it is unlikely there were more than 12.

Loading the two vessels at Gothenburg was a time-consuming task that Minuit supervised. The merchandise and supplies Blommaert shipped from Amsterdam had to be integrated with purchases made in Sweden. For instance, Minuit bought 500 bricks in Gothenburg from Hans Macklier which he knew would be needed for chimneys and fireplaces in any buildings he erected.[12] He knew what it meant to be without bricks, having experienced that need on Manhattan Island at a time before there were brickmakers or kilns in the colony. He also took aboard two barrels of wheat and two barrels of barley, oats, and rye for use as seeds. The probability is that he also took seeds for peas, beans, and cabbages so that vegetable gardens could be planted. Spades, hoes, shovels, and other farming tools were included among the supplies, as well as casks of wine. The Crown supplied 30 muskets for the soldiers and over 3,000 pounds of powder; the admiralty supplied goods worth 1711 R.D.[13]

The selection of trade goods to be used in bartering for furs was of paramount importance. Obtaining furs depended upon having the kind of goods that the natives wanted, and their needs changed over periods of time. For instance, in their initial contacts with European traders the Indians expressed little interest in guns, but a time soon came when guns, flint, lead, and powder were much in demand. Unsuccessful efforts were made to deny them such weapons because of the possible consequences.

Blommaert had a better understanding of the fur trade than Spiring or Admiral Fleming who had no practical knowledge, but he had never personally conducted negotiations with the Indians. Minuit was the only one of the principals who had actually bargained with the natives, and he learned it was not simply a matter of having a random selection of glass beads and baubles. Certain kinds of tools and implements were in demand, whereas others were not. Cloth had to be of a specified quality and color, or the Indians were reluctant to pay a high price for it in terms of skins.

Fur trading was a highly competitive business, and Dutch, English, and French traders were doing their best to dominate the market. If traders from one nation failed to provide the merchandise most in demand, the furs were diverted to a rival who had a better understanding of native needs. Minuit realized that with the keen European competition it was then a seller's market, and goodwill had to be maintained with the tribal chiefs, as well as the native hunters and trappers, by periodically giving them presents.

Trade goods in the cargo of the *Kalmar Nyckel* included "several hundred axes, hatchets, adzes, several hundred knives, dozens of tobacco pipes, mirrors, looking-glasses, gilded chains, and finger-rings, combs, earrings and other ornaments."[14] To this should be added jews harps which enabled an untrained Indian to make musical sounds, and copper and brass kettles which were in demand among the Indian women.

The European steel knives, axes, and hatchets had sharper cutting edges than the flint knives and stone axes and celts used by the Indian tribes. Iron hoes were more efficient than hoes made of a deer scapula. Metal kettles and cooking pots were unbreakable in contrast to the friable, sun-dried, clay vessels made by the Indian women. The Lenape and Minquas were essentially in a stone age before the Europeans introduced superior products to these primitive people whose material culture was based on artifacts of stone, bone, shell, clay, and wood.

To a people having no knowledge of woven fabrics, who dressed in animal skins, the Dutch duffel cloth (named from Duffel, a suburb of Antwerp, where it was made) was the most wanted European commodity during Minuit's time. A few years later guns and gunpowder took first position. The coarsely woven duffel cloth was rolled on a bolt, and in negotiations with the Indians the cloth was unrolled and specified quantities were measured and scissored off. Indian males wore it around the upper parts of their bodies like a toga, leaving one arm uncovered. It could also be worn as a shawl around the shoulders, or tied around the loins like a girdle with flaps in the front and back. Indian women used the cloth to make wrap-around skirts, and it served as a light blanket to cover children in their beds. At first the Indians were fascinated with the duffel cloth dyed red, but when the hunter learned that this color revealed his presence to the animal he was stalking, more somber colors like brown and dark blue came into demand.

The young Swedish engineer Peter Lindeström, writing in 1654, explains how some of the traders tricked the Indians:

> When the Christians measure the frieze [duffels] for the savage, they measure it for the savage on the edge, the savage taking hold of a corner of the frieze and the Christians on the edge, whereupon they pull the hardest they are able, stretching thus the ell for the savage so that he for three ells barely gets more than two; which the savage thinks should be thus, and does not understand himself cheated in this.[15]

Minuit knew that priority had to be given to the duffel cloth especially in demand among the Lenape and Minquas. The exact quantity taken aboard the *Kalmar Nyckel* is not known, but it was in excess of the 2,748 ½ yards which Blommaert reported he had woven for the expedition. Even if Dutch "ells" were meant, which was only ¾ of an English yard, by linear measurement this quantity of cloth unrolled would be almost a mile long, and even in compact bolts it required considerable cargo space.

No women or children passengers were aboard the ships in the first expedition, the personnel consisting of sailors, ships' officers, soldiers, servants, and craftsmen. All were paid employes either by the New Sweden Company or the Swedish government. No complete listing of their names has yet been found. The likelihood is that the *Kalmar Nyckel* was manned by 30 or 40 sailors, and she carried from 24 to 28 soldiers. Most of the sailors were Dutch and most of the soldiers were Swedish. The nationality of a man could not be determined by his name, because many men having Scandinavian names were actually Dutch and vice versa. Spelling by both Dutch and Swedes was careless and inconsistent.

The *Fogel Grip* may have been manned by 12 or 15 sailors and she probably carried a small complement of soldiers. This is speculative in the absence of more definitive data, although the records indicate that she carried cannon, but the number is unknown.

The names of 17 or 18 members of the first expedition are known from references made in letters, reports, and other reliable sources which the author has carefully checked. Minuit, of course, approximately at the age of 48, was the nominal leader of the expedition, although each vessel had its own skipper. As indicated in the opening chapter, Jan Hindricksen van der Water was the captain of the *Kalmar Nyckel*, and Michel Symonssen, from Sardam, aged 54, another Dutchman, was the first mate. (His name is also given as Michiel Symonsz). Jacob Evertssen Sandelin, a Scotchman aged 38, was the second mate. It was not unusual for experienced seamen from the British Isles to find employment on Dutch vessels, and Sandelin figured as the mate of the *Charitas* on the third Swedish expedition in 1641-42.

Andrian Jöransen, captain of the *Grip*, was assisted by Andres Lucassen, the upper boatswain. He, too, was a Dutchman who had been in America in the employ of the West India Company, and was engaged by Minuit as the Indian interpreter. During the voyage he was succeeded as upper boatswain by Peter Johanssen, a Dutchman from Beemster, aged 27.

Others who have been identified were Johan Jochimssen from Cappel, in Schleswig-Holstein, aged 30, a gunner on the *Kalmar Nyckel*. Måns Nilsson Kling, an experienced army man, was the commander of the soldiers in the expedition; he was either a Swede or a Finn. Hendrick Huygen, aged about 29, Minuit's capable nephew from Wesel, was in charge of supplies holding a key position as the comissary or storekeeper.

The reader will recall that his father Jan Huygen, who married Minuit's wife's sister Sibylle Raet, served Minuit in a similar capacity at Fort Amsterdam. Hendrick Huygen's appointment in the Swedish expedition was not by chance, and Minuit undoubtedly had something to do with it, although time has obscured the details. A German boy named Gotfried Harmer accompanied Huygen in the role of an apprentice-servant. He was referred to as a nephew of Minuit's, and as Hendrick Huygen's cousin.[16] Actually his blood ties were through Minuit's lineage since he was the grandson of Minuit's sister Sarah who married Daniel Hermer (or Harmar), which makes him Minuit's grandnephew. Minuit may have also had an influence on Gotfried's employment in the first expedition, but these particulars are also missing. Minuit may have believed that his potential plans for settling his war-scarred countrymen in New Sweden would be aided by having Huygen and Harmer see the land he had chosen in America as the site of the colony.

Herrman Andersson, Johan Svensson, and Sander Clerck, were three of the Swedish sailors, and Clas Janssen was one of the party who decided to remain in the colony as a freeman. This means he became an independent farmer or artisan not beholden to the company as a paid employe. The two barber-surgeons in the expedition were Timen Stiddem from Gothenburg, Sweden, and Hans Janeke from Konigsberg, Prussia. Stiddem was the ancestor of a prominent family destined to become extensive landowners at Wilmington. William Loury may also have been an expedition member, either a sailor or soldier, although the evidence is less clear than it is for those cited above.

As plans for the expedition reached the final stages, Minuit was given a letter to be read to the skippers, as well as the soldiers and sailors, regarding their conduct. The letter contained 32 articles, and its salient excerpts included the following provisions:[17]

The sailors and officers in every instance should obey their commander. In the event of disobedience, the offender was to lose his monthly pay.

Officers and men were to keep good watch day and night and have their arms in readiness to fight if necessary.

When they reached the New World everyone was forbidden from carrying on trade with the Indians on his own account, and was prohibited from carrying trade goods belonging to private merchants. (This was to protect the trade interest of the New Sweden Company.)

Stealing by members of the expedition, either on board ship, or when the vessels landed, would be severely punished.

No fighting between sailors during the voyage would be permitted, and drunkenness was strictly prohibited. Anyone who broke the rule was to be placed in irons for three days. Card playing and shooting crap with dice, or other games of chance, were forbidden.

Prayers were to be conducted morning and evening aboard ship, and anyone who was absent from the services without permission was to be fined six stuivers. (The records do not state who conducted religious services on the *Kalmar Nyckel*, but as a deacon in the Reformed Church, in the absence of an ordained pastor, Minuit probably assumed the responsibility.)

The secret instructions which Blommaert gave to Minuit when the latter left for Stockholm was no. 3 on the list of documents he took to Sweden with him. One Swedish historian believes the instructions may have been written by Minuit himself.[18] The contents clearly indicate that the author (or one of the authors) was familiar with the geography of the New Netherland, particularly the Delaware River valley. Possibly it was a joint effort in which both Blommaert and Minuit participated, and since it was also intended for the eyes of Oxenstierna and Admiral Fleming, Spiring probably approved it. None of the Swedish leaders knew enough about the geography of the New World to prepare such instructions although they may have suggested amendments relative to naming some of the places on the itinerary, and how Minuit should react if he encountered French, English, Dutch, or Spanish vessels. An English translation of the lengthy instructions consumes almost fourteen printed pages.[19] Some of the key points are cited below.

King Gustavus Adolphus (1594-1632) whose religious zeal made him widely known as a champion and defender of the Lutheran faith. Reorganized Sweden's military, political, and economic systems. Killed in the Battle of Lützen in Germany defending Protestantism. Although New Sweden did not come into existence until after his death, he added the *Kalmar Nyckel* to the Swedish fleet during his reign. (Courtesy of the Historical Society of Pennsylvania)

Axel Oxenstierna (1583-1654), became chancellor of Sweden in 1612, and after King Gustavus Adolphus's death was one of the regents ruling the kingdom. A sagacious statesman he was the virtual ruler until Christina ascended the throne. He fully supported the New Sweden colony and approved Peter Minuit's original recommendations. (Courtesy of the Historical Society of Pennsylvania)

Samuel Blommaert (1583-1654), prominent Dutch merchant, a director of the Dutch West India Company, and one of the Swanendael
patroons. In 1636 he became a Swedish business "consul" in
Amsterdam, and was a leading figure in planning the 1638 voyage
of the *Kalmar Nyckel* with Peter Minuit. (Courtesy Stichting Iconographisch Bureau, the Hague, Holland)

Miniature oil painting of Baron Peter Spiring Silfverkrona, son of a wealthy Dutchman, who represented
Sweden in Holland beginning in 1635. He supported Peter Minuit and Samuel Blommaert in obtaining Swedish financial support for the *Kalmar
Nyckel's* voyage. (Courtesy National Swedish Art
Museums, Stockholm)

CLAS FLEMMING.
Gubernestä my: Maijp: och sira Rikes Rad
Öuerstatthallare Amiral. Född d: 6 Mart: 1592.

Admiral Klas Larsson Fleming (1592-1644), a Finn, who as president of the Board of Trade, strongly supported Minuit's plans to found a New Sweden. (Courtesy Stockholm City Museum)

Peter Minuit's alleged purchase of Manhattan Island by the American painter William Ranney (1813-1857). The characters are imaginative since no likeness of Minuit exists. The Indian clothing and hairdress are inaccurate for the time and place, and log cabins (shown in background) were non-existent on Manhattan Island when Manhattan was purchased from the Indians. Painting is undated but executed before 1857. (Courtesy of Rutgers University)

Queen Christina (1626-1689) painted in 1638 the year Peter Minuit built and named the fort in her honor at Wilmington. She was then 12 years of age and apparently dressed for a special court occasion. Note delicate lace on her gown, precious pearl necklace, and feather (ostrich?) fan. (Courtesy Swedish Art Museum, Stockholm)

Copy of Peter Minuit's original letter in the Dutch language dated June 15, 1636 proposing a settlement be made in America to be called "Nova Sweediae" (New Sweden). See chapter 4 above for an English translation of the letter. (Courtesy Swedish Royal Archives, Stockholm)

All of the known letters written by Minuit were in Dutch. It is unlikely that he could read and write Swedish, and doubtful that he could speak Swedish fluently. Most Swedish officials at the time were fluent in Dutch.

Plaque at Wesel, Germany in Peter Minuit's honor which reads:
Peter Minuit
Dem Sohne Unserer Stadt
Der 1626 Die Weltstadt
New York
Und 1638 Die Amerikanische
Stadt Wilmington Gründete
Freely translated this means, "Peter Minuit, the son of our city who founded the metropolis of New York in 1626, and in 1638 the American city of Wilmington." (Photo by Allen C. Rawl)

Peter Minuit's signature. Pronounced Min-wee, meaning "midnight" in French, all of his known letters were written in Dutch. His Dutch and Swedish contemporaries often misspelled his name, such as Menwe, Minnewitz, Minnewit, etc.

Minuit did not live to see Christina ascend to the Swedish throne in 1644 as an educated queen aged 18 who devoured theology, classical languages, literature, and politics. Her court became a center for scholars and artists. She is shown in the company of the French philosopher René Descartes (standing at table at right) who visited the Swedish court in 1649. (Courtesy National Swedish Art Museums, Stockholm)

In this first encounter between the Swedes and the Lenape
at "the Rocks" in Wilmington, the artist Stanley Arthurs por-
trays Minuit as a leader wearing the scarf (baldric) of authority, right hand supporting a staff. Aware that no portrait of
Minuit exists, the artist, dedicated to historical realism, skill-
fully avoided a full face view. Andress Lucassen, Minuit's
translator, greets the chief Mattahorn whose upraised hand
denotes friendship. Note copper kettle at bottom right containing gifts for the Indians. (Courtesy of the Permanent Collections, University of Delaware. Original oil painting on display
in Memorial Hall, Newark, Delaware)

Crowd gathers for dedicatory ceremony at "the Rocks," present Fort Christina Park, Wilmington, June 27, 1938. Prince Bertil arrived in launch in foreground from the *Kungsholm* at anchor in the Delaware River to present monument at right to President Franklin D. Roosevelt, a gift from the Swedish people. The author was among the reporters. (Courtesy the Historical Society of Delaware)

Opposite Page: Aerial view of Wilmington in 1938, the white dot at upper right indicating approximate location of "the Rocks" where Peter Minuit landed in the *Kalmar Nyckel* in 1638. The Christina merges with Delaware River at top right beyond junction with the Brandywine. The former Pennsylvania R.R. tracks (now Amtrak) follow the curve in the Christina. Bridge in foreground leads to Market Street and cluster of tall buildings downtown. The city has undergone many changes since this photo was taken.

Brought from Sweden in sections, monument sculpted by Carl Milles (1875-1955) with replica of *Kalmar Nyckel* was re-assembled by Swedish workmen starting in mid-May, 1638, and was permanently in place in time for the dedicatory services on June 27. Milles, born in Sweden, became a United States citizen in 1945. (Courtesy Historical Society of Delaware)

Above scene in bas relief on one side of monument depicts King
Gustavus Adolphus and a stylized view of Fort Christina with the
inscription "First Permanent Settlement In the Delaware Valley."
Gustavus Adolphus is symbolically holding the *Kalmar Nyckel* in
his right hand. Milles, the sculptor, was an assistant to Rodin in
Paris and later taught at Cranbrook Academy of Art in Michigan.
He must have known that the king had been dead five years before
the New Sweden Company was formed and the *Kalmar Nyckel*
commissioned for the first voyage.

Minuit was instructed to run around England and Scotland after leaving Gothenburg, and after crossing the Atlantic he was to land at the "Ille de Sable," winds and weather permitting. Sable Island, as it is now known, is located approximately 100 miles off the southeastern coast of Nova Scotia. When he arrived at the island, Minuit was ordered to have the ship's carpenter reassemble the sloop carried by the *Kalmar Nyckel* and use it to explore the island waters. If the island was not occupied, and he found it suitable for populating and planting by Europeans, he was supposed to take possession, erect a stone marker bearing the Swedish coat of arms, and name it Christina Island in the queen's honor. Blommaert conceived of it as a stopping-off place for Swedish ships later sailing back and forth to the mainland, and also a place where tariffs could be collected from vessels returning to Europe with fish obtained in waters off Newfoundland.

Minuit was given an alternate course for the first leg of the voyage in the event he was unable to reach the Sable Islands; namely, he was to sail to the West Indies by way of the Caribbean, and from there:

> You *shall then sail away secretly to the South River without touching the North River [Hudson]* and *run to the Minquas Kill*, doing all in your power, by means of gifts, to barter with the savages so that everywhere in the land you make known that you have come to trade with them in good fellowship.[20]

The italicized words can be interpreted to mean that the Dutch governor-general at Manhattan Island should know as little as possible about the Swedish expedition, especially its destination. The instructions further emphasized this in another line, "You shall also shun the limits of New Netherland in order not to become involved in any quarrel with the West India Company." Blommaert continued to withhold information about the voyage from his fellow directors, although in a letter written in 1640, he intimated the directors did not object "as long as Minuit stayed outside the limits of New Netherland."[21] The issue was where were these bounds?

Minuit's concepts were different from those of the West India Company, whose charter gave it a monopoly for 24 years to trade in specified foreign waters including the full sweep of the North and South American coasts.

An important line in the instructions stated that "in the Minques kill we intend to take possession," which leaves no doubt about the destination of the vessels. Furthermore, if Minuit believed it advisable to do so, he was authorized "to place on the Minquas kill, at a point which is naturally strong for defense, a lodge or house in which the people may dwell who remain there, close to the sloop." It was left to his judgement whether or not it was advisable "to fortify a little the house that is erected on the land in the Minques Kill."

To make certain of a secure possession of the land, the instructions read that the Swedish coat of arms should be raised on the Minquas Kill after the land was purchased from the Indians. Furthermore, a deposition should be signed by the officers in the expedition to the effect that no Europeans were living on the land Minuit claimed for Sweden.

The two vessels never reached Sable Island; in fact, it is unlikely that Minuit would have risked the safety of the ships and crews by heading so far north in dangerous waters. When the instructions were written, Blommaert fully expected the ships to leave Sweden in the spring or summer of 1637, which would have permitted visiting Sable Island in favorable weather. The two ships did not leave Gothenburg until sometime in November 1637, and that was not the time of year to follow a course to Newfoundland waters and the "graveyard of the Atlantic" which sailors called the sea surrounding Sable Island.

After conferring with his officers, Minuit decided to follow a direct course to the West Indies and from there to the South River. Hopefully he would reach the Minquas Kill in time to alert the Indians to his presence prior to their winter hunting trips. This would guarantee obtaining the maximum number of pelts in the spring and summer of 1638 for the return voyage to Gothenburg.

The instructions reiterated the importance of conducting religious services regularly aboard the vessels. A prayer should be read and a Psalm sung every morning and evening, "and on Sunday a chapter from the New Testament read."

Unfortunately, no motion picture or TV cameras were there to record the departure from Gothenburg, the *Kalmar Nyckel* leading the way in the familiar waters of the harbor her sails yielding to the wind. There must have been wives and sweethearts tearfully waving their goodbyes to some of the Swedish sailors and soldiers, but those seamen hired in Amsterdam had no loved ones in Gothenburg to see them off. Minuit was alone, too, his wife in Kleve, and if his nephew Hendrick Huygen had a wife, she too was living in their homeland. Thoughts of the war-torn Rhineland must have flashed through both Minuit's and Huygen's minds as they headed out to sea. During the voyage they may have discussed how they would take specific steps on their return to help the war-weary farmers of Klever Land to find new homes and new opportunities in New Sweden. That would come with the second expedition — the immediate problem was to secure lands in America for Sweden without running afoul of the Dutch West India Company, and to return with furs and tobacco for the benefit of their sponsors.

Chapter 5 Notes

1. Johnson believes Fleming was appointed the director, *SS* 1:107, but Dahlgren can find no proof of this, Dahlgren and Norman, *Rise and Fall of New Sweden*, p. 5.
2. *SS* 1:111.
3. *Blommaert Letters*, No. 28, Sept. 9, 1637.
4. Letter No. 27.
5. Letter No. 29, Sept. 29, 1637.
6. *SS* 2:758, n. 7.
7. D. Hj. Borjeson, *Stockholm's Segelsjöfart Minnesskrift 1732-1932,* (Stockholm, 1932), p. 166. Mrs. Marianne Eckerström Mackenzie made the English translation of the passage.
8. Information from Carl H. Friberg of Saltsjöbaden, Sweden, personal letter Nov. 14, 1987.
9. This information was obtained from an undated typed description kindly supplied by Manne Dunge, Curator, Sjöfartsmuseet in Gothenburg. The translation was made by Marianne Eckerström Mackenzie. Johnson states that in 1632 the *Kalmar Nyckel* was purchased for 27,898 dal-

ers, but the author is unable to reconcile this with other citations, *SS* 1:78.

10. From typed description supplied by Manne Dunge.
11. P.0. Bäckstrom, *Svenska Flottans Historia*, Stockholm, p. 396.
12. See copy of ledger page, *SS* 1: op. p. 194.
13. *SS* 1:105.
14. *SS* 1:112.
15. Lindeström, Peter, *Geographia Americae*, trans. Amandus Johnson (Philadelphia: Swedish Colonial Society, 1922), p. 226.
16. C.A. Weslager, "The City of Amsterdam's Colony on the Delaware 1656-1664: With Unpublished Dutch Notarial Abstracts," Part 2, *Delaware History* 20: 80, Fall-Winter 1982.
17. The cooperation of Helena Welin-Berger of the Riksarkivet in Stockholm is acknowledged in supplying a photocopy of the document entitled *Articul Bief, etc.*
18. Carl K.S. Sprinchorn, "The History of the Colony of New Sweden," trans. G.B. Keen, *Pennsylvania Magazine of History and Biography* 8:254 fn., 1884.
19. *Weslager, 1961*, pp. 168-181.
20. *Ibid.*, 171-72.
21. *Blommaert Letters*, No. 36, January 28, 1640.

6. The *Kalmar Nyckel* Sails

The crews of the *Kalmar Nyckel* and the *Grip* had no difficulty bringing the two vessels through the Skagerak from Gothenburg where the depth of the water, the winds, and tides were familiar to their officers. But the experienced sailors aboard the vessels knew that even skilled Dutch captains could not predict what awaited them in the extremely cold November winds as they entered the North Sea. It was no secret that Minuit, despite the high regard in which he was held by the crews, was a stranger to these northern waters, and depended upon the judgements of Captains van der Water and Jöransen. The two Dutch skippers had navigated the sea lanes between Gothenburg and the Dutch ports, but they probably had doubts about plotting a course from Sweden to the Atlantic around the British Isles which Blommaert had instructed Minuit to follow to avoid pirates. This meant sailing directly across the North Sea and then veering southeast into possible storms before reaching the Atlantic.

The North Sea, 700 miles long and 400 miles wide, was subject to unusual tides. One tide wave came northward through the English Channel and the Straits of Dover, and another moved southward across the Norwegian Channel to the Danish coast. The numerous fresh water rivers emptying into it — the Thames, Rhine, Elbe, Weser, Ems, Scheldt, and others — dilute its salt, making it prone to ice formation. Aggravated by winter winds bringing sleet and snow, sailing vessels often had difficulty holding to a charted course.

What course the vessels followed is not known, because Minuit's log book is among the missing documents containing data about the expedition.[1] From accounts told later by members of the crew, the ships encountered strong headwinds and were battered by violent storms in the North Sea. They tossed and turned in the turbulence, and the storm caused them to become separated and they lost visual contact. What first appeared as a short-lived winter squall became a raging storm. The crew on the *Kalmar Nyckel* thought that the smaller *Grip* had been engulfed by the towering waves, and Captain Jöransen on the *Grip* may have believed that the *Kalmar Nyckel* had gone to the bottom.

The crude navigational instruments on both ships — the magnetic compass, the astrolab, and the sounding lead — were as useless as tiller and rudder in the roaring northern gales and angry seas. Minuit was almost prophetic when he stated in his famous letter written more than a year before that "the best time to set sail would be the sooner the better." He was then thinking of sailing across a placid sea warmed by summer sunshine. Now it was too late except to bundle up, double his scarf around his face and neck, and pray for divine protection for his men and his ship as they struggled to remain afloat.

How the *Kalmar Nyckel* was able to survive the fury of the angry seas remains unanswered, but early in December by dead reckoning she came into the protection of the harbor at Texel on the dying winds of the frightful storm. Dozens of other sailing craft were lying at anchor in the Dutch port, many suffering storm damage. After the *Kalmar Nyckel* was carefully examined, she was found leaking at her seams; she had lost her main mast, damaged her prow, and lost her headknee

— the forepart of the prow.[2] The canvas of her spritsail and sprit topsail were torn, but she was still afloat and all hands were accounted for.

Wonder of wonders, the *Grip*, believed to have been lost, arrived a week later, long after she had been given up, badly in need of repairs, but still navigable. Evidently Minuit had made prearrangements for a rendezvous in Holland if the vessels were unable to break through storms to the Atlantic. What a happy reunion that must have been for officers, soldiers, and crews of both ships to find they were all alive, and what a relief for Minuit who took very seriously the responsibility for the personnel in his command. He must have been especially proud of the *Kalmar Nyckel* as she rode erect at anchor in the roadstead at Texel ready to obey his commands despite the damage she had suffered. It was the kind of attachment between a man and his ship that Melville's fictional Captain Ahab would find on the *Pequod* centuries later as he pursued the white whale, Moby Dick.

Minuit lost no time in breaking the news of the delay to Blommaert in Amsterdam who promptly notified Spiring at the Hague, who in turn relayed the information to Admiral Fleming in Stockholm. What should be done? Should they await several weeks for Fleming's reply? Did the delay and the added expense mean that the project should be aborted? Repairing the two vessels was only one element in the added costs; the crews had to be paid while the vessels were at anchor, and the provisions already consumed by the crews had to be replenished. There isn't the slightest indication in the records of any feeling of defeat on Minuit's part. From his point of view there was no need to lose further time by awaiting a reply from Stockholm. He wanted to continue across the Atlantic despite the taunting whistle of the wind.

Blommaert and Spiring agreed. The *Kalmar Nyckel* underwent repairs at Texel, and to conserve time, the *Grip* went to nearby Medemblik to be made seaworthy again. In retrospect, it is apparent that this delay and added expense could have been avoided if Amsterdam instead of Gothenburg had been selected as the base of operations. That's where most of the cargo originated and where most of the sailors were hired. Of course, this would have aroused the suspicions of the West India Company at a crucial time when the Swedish secret voyage was being closely guarded. Minuit was still apprehensive that the two vessels flying Swedish flags undergoing repairs in Dutch ports would arouse curiosity and cause questions to be asked in the offices of the Dutch West India Company. Above all he did not want the information to reach the directors of the Company that his destination was the Minquas Kill in the South River. He did not want to argue the question about whether this was *in* the New Netherland or simply adjacent to it, which would open up Pandora's box and further delay the voyage.

Imagine Minuit's uneasiness when he chanced to meet an old friend and one of the first directors of the Amsterdam Chamber, the rich patroon and diamond merchant Kiliaen van Rensselaer. History does not reveal how or why their paths crossed. Perhaps they encountered each other on one of the many bridges that cross the city's canals when Minuit was hurrying to Blommaert's office, or in one of the shops in Amsterdam where he was buying supplies for use aboard the *Kalmar Nyckel* being repaired at Texel. It was certainly not a meeting that Minuit sought, but it was a propitious one for van Rensselaer who was trying to find transportation for six young Dutchmen he had recruited as employes in his patroonship at Rensselaerswyck on the Hudson River at present Albany.

Growth of his colony had been slow and van Rensselaer was doing his utmost to increase its productivity by sending farmers who could raise grains and other agricultural products and export them for sale in Holland. His problem was to induce settlers to go to the colony and work for daily wages under the supervision of his local overseer. Young healthy

Dutchmen were still reluctant to leave their homeland even though the patroon advertised that there were unusual opportunities in America. Of approximately 50 families who had gone to Rensselaerswyck since the colony was established in 1630, some came from England, Norway, and various German principalities, but Holland was slow to respond.

He told Minuit that one of the six young Dutchmen he had recruited was his grandnephew, Arent van Curler, aged 18, to whom he generally referred to as "cousin." He had assured his nephew that after he gained experience in the colony he would be placed in charge as overseer with a rare opportunity of winning fame and fortune as the colony expanded. The others were Elbert Albertsen, a weaver from Nieukerck [present Nijkerk?] aged 16; Claes Jansen, a tailor from Nieukerck aged 17; Gerrit Hendricksz, a shoemaker from Nieukerck aged 15; and two farmers, Ghysbert Arentsen from Bunnick aged 22; and Jacob Ariaensz, from Utrecht aged 25.[3] The spellings of these names vary, and van Rensselaer spelled them differently almost each time he wrote the name!

It was not the patroon's intention that the weaver, tailor, and carpenter would pursue their own trades in the colony. He expected all of them to become farmers, and concentrate on growing the high-profit American product then widely in demand in Holland — tobacco.[4] Van Rensselaer had a small vessel of his own, but it was not then in service, and there was no passenger space on any of the West India Company's vessels getting ready to depart for New Netherland. Van Rensselaer was anxious to get the young men aboard a ship before they changed their minds, and his meeting with Minuit was like a godsend.

Minuit did not attempt to conceal from van Rensselaer the obvious fact that his two ships were being renovated for a transatlantic voyage, but he was guarded in his conversation and was especially careful not to reveal his destination. He merely indicated that he was headed for "the Virginias," a

term that might have applied to any place along the Atlantic
seaboard north of Spanish Florida. That answer seemed to
satisfy van Rensselaer, and he offered to pay Minuit to take
his six employes with him in the expectation that once they
reached "the Virginias" some way would be found for their
transportation to his colony on the Hudson River. Van Rensselaer makes this clear in a letter he wrote on May 7, 1638 to
Willem Kieft who had been appointed the West India Company's new governor-general of New Netherland the previous
September. He replaced Wouter van Twiller who succeeded
Minuit. The letter reads in part as follows:

> As shortly after your honor's departure from the Texel my small
> vessel arrived here from New Netherland bringing me advice of
> some things needed by my people there and it so happened that the
> ship *de Calmer Slutel* [Dutch for *Kalmar Nyckel*], commander pitter
> miniet* in the service of the crown of Sweden, was obliged to seek
> shelter here at the Texel on account of storms, I did not want to
> neglect this opportunity, though in midwinter and in freezing
> weather, of supplying my people [at Rensselaerswyck] as far as
> possible with necessaries and of improving the condition of New
> Netherland as much as possible as to population, and, trusting to
> God's mercy, I have also sent over six persons, though his destina-
> tion was unknown to me. I could make out only this much, that he
> expected to go to Virginia, from which region I have asked him to
> try to find opportunity to send my goods and people to the Com-
> pany's settlement.[5]

Although it appears to have been an imposition to ask the
commander of an already crowded ship to make room for six
additional men, van Rensselaer also sent a note to Minuit at
Texel dated December 25, 1637 that he was going to ship some
merchandise in a lighter from Amsterdam which he hoped
Minuit would also take to America for him. By then the two
vessels had been repaired and were awaiting favorable eastern
winds to resume the voyage. He listed the goods as follows
which were requisitioned by his overseer at Rensselaerswyck:

---

*Van Rensselaer in other letters spells the name Pieter Minnewiet,
Pietter Minuijt, Pietter Minuytt, etc.

A B C   being three wooden boxes, contents according to manifest
D E F G H   being five packing boxes
N.B. I   one ditto chest also included in the manifest which could
not be got ready and will be sent herewith or later according to the time available
K L   two barrels of salt (*smaltonnen*)
M   a long box with firelocks; herewith, ordered by *hendrick Trip*, a
keg with 50 lb of fine gunpowder
N   a large wicker hamper with wooden utensils
0   being five winnowing baskets tied together; a small barrel with
grapevines for the Commander Minuijt[6]
[winnowing baskets were used to separate chaff from wheat. The
grapevines were intended as a present for Minuit to plant.]

Van Rensselaer stated in his note that he had paid Captain
van der Water, who was then in Amsterdam, 220:10 florins as
board and transportation for the six passengers, and also to cover
the cost of shipping the merchandise on the *Kalmar Nyckel*.

It required Thursday and Friday, December 24 and 25, to
load the lighter which sailed from Amsterdam on Saturday,
December 26. The lighter did not reach Texel until Monday,
December 28, a two-day trip. On Tuesday, December 29, two
days before the *Kalmar Nyckel* sailed, van Rensselaer wrote a
second letter to Minuit which was delivered by his grandnephew when he boarded the ship almost at the last minute
with his companions. It reads in part as follows:

Heer Commandeur: The bearer of this letter my cousin Arent
van Corler, sailing to my colony as assistant, is recommended to
you to accomodate him as much as your honor's situation will allow.
I trust that your honor will not fail herein but show me friendship. I
should also be much pleased, inasmuch as he is still young and
inexperienced, if you had a little instruction given to him in the
process of ship's bookkeeping as well as in the keeping of land
accounts, as his master Jacob Planck [van Rensselaer's agent in the
colony] with whom he will be, is not too expert in these matters
himself. He takes with him a mate's chest marked on the inside No. 1,
in which there are some Hainault and grass scythes and other hard-
ware which I could not put into the lighter which sailed on Saturday
[from Amsterdam] and therefore did not reach your honor till yester-

day. This small chest you will please add to the other items mentioned in my last letter, and under supervision or in the keeping of my aforesaid cousin have brought to the *manatans* [Manhattan Island] by the best means you can find. With him go the following young men engaged for my colony [names of the five young men listed].

Loaded also one barrel of pitch, well hooped, f 18 [and] 2 barrels of tar, together f 15.[7]

Van Rensselaer's request that Minuit give his "nephew" accounting lessons during the voyage seems to have been stretching friendship almost to the breaking point, but the older man was grateful enough to tell Minuit that in return for the favors "you must command me wherever I can do you a service or kindness." He doubtless meant what he said, and Minuit was probably sincere in obliging an old friend.

On Thursday, December 31, the two Swedish ships, along with 150 other vessels that had been awaiting favorable winds, put out to sea.[8] The majority were armed merchant vessels, large and small, some destined for the Straits of Gibraltar, others for the East Indies via the Cape of Good Hope, and still others for Brazil where the Dutch West India Company was fighting a losing cause to unseat the Portuguese and control the profitable sugar market. Most of these vessels must have sailed through the English Channel, the strength of their numbers deterring attacks by pirates in the Straits of Dover. Probably the *Kalmar Nyckel* and the *Grip* followed the channel route, but the loss of Minuit's log leaves this question unresolved. Nor is anything known about the voyage across the Atlantic, but if the vessels arrived in the South River in mid-March of 1638, which is the generally accepted date, they lost no time after leaving Texel on December 31. They must have made the voyage from Holland to the Minquas Kill in 75 or 80 days which was good time. Unless the ships tarried somewhere enroute, the six uninvited passengers, the only ones whose voyage was paid for, were still aboard the *Kalmar Nyckel*. If so, some way had to be found to get them to Albany, but Minuit had immediate problems with higher priority.

After ascending the Delaware River, as discussed in the opening chapter, Minuit selected "the Rocks" on the Minquas Kill as the most likely site for the headquarters of the Swedish colony. It might be asked why he did not choose a site on the banks of the Delaware River instead of going two miles upstream on a tributary. Ships of the Dutch West India Company sailed back and forth between New Amsterdam and Fort Nassau situated on the opposite bank of the Delaware River at present Gloucester, New Jersey. See Map 4. He deliberately selected a location not visible to these ships to avoid any trouble with the Dutch. It was also important for him to make certain that there were no Europeans settled along the Minquas Kill. This was part of the strategy in securing ownership for the Swedes; he wanted to avoid a premature confrontation with the English who may have found their way from Maryland to the headwaters of the Minquas Kill.[9]

Neither the *Kalmar Nyckel* nor the *Grip* were suited for exploring the Minquas Kill and its tributaries, because of the uncertainty of its depth above the head of tidewater. The ebb and flow of the tide facilitated traveling between "the Rocks" and the fall line, but the ships might have grounded in shallow water farther upstream. Minuit ordered the ship's carpenters to remove the disassembled sloop from aboard the *Kalmar Nyckel* and make it ready for exploration. It was a small sailing craft having one or two masts, possibly comparable to a ketch or yawl which could accommodate five or six men. It must have been equipped with oars for use if it became necessary to row in shallow water.

The sloop went on a number of forays up the creek and the men made landings at different locations to explore the terrain. They probably saw sites of deserted Indian hunting camps, but their main concern was to make certain that no European houses or trading posts had been built along the banks during the six years that had elapsed since Minuit had been in New Netherland. The English settled Lord Baltimore's Maryland colony on the Potomac in 1634 two years after Minuit had gone back to Holland, and he was unsure of the extent of their settlement.

Going upstream from "the Rocks" where the two larger vessels remained behind at anchor, the creek swerved south, then made a wide horseshoe curve eastward, and turned back on itself to ramble toward the west. It was a sluggish, slow-moving stream, which eased over its banks to form extensive marshes in the lowlands. These swampy areas were stippled with the grassy mounds of dozens of muskrat houses, swamp-loving cattails, pickerel weeds, calamus, and numerous species of shore birds. Above the present town of Newport the creek was joined by its main tributaries then unnamed, but known today as White Clay Creek, Red Clay Creek, Mill Creek, and Pike Creek.

Minuit, to be sure, accompanied the men on one or more of these explorations. He was interested in seeing for himself how the creek coursed beyond the head of tidewater in the vicinity of the general area now called Cooch's Bridge. Here the stream narrows having well-defined banks, and its smaller fresh water tributaries straggle to spring heads in the western woods. It was in this vicinity, at the base of a promontory later called Iron Hill, where the Minquas Indian trail serpentined overland from the Head of Elk. This was one of the natural routes for English settlers in Maryland to reach the Minquas Kill following the old Indian portage path.

We know from a deposition made by four of the men accompanying Minuit, who later signed an affidavit before a Dutch notary in Amsterdam that:

> they made their presence known with all kinds of signs, both by the firing of cannon and otherwise, and also sailed several miles into the same [Minquas] river, and went into the country, but neither found nor observed any sign or vestige of Christian people; whereupon the above mentioned Director Peter Minuit requested and *caused the nations of people to whom the land really belonged to come before him, whom he then asked, if they wished to sell the river, with all the*

land lying about there, as many days' journey as they would request.
This they agreed to with the common consent of the nations.[10]

The italicized words are important for an understanding of how Minuit intended to obtain legal claim for Swedish owner-ship of the land he had selected, even though he knew that the Swedes had not previously explored or settled there. Both Dutch and English claimed lands along the Atlantic coast either by right of prior discovery, or because they had first settled or cultivated parts of the territory. To the English, for example, the land they called Virginia which extended as far as New England, was considered the property of the English Crown by right of the discoveries of John Cabot, an explorer in English employ. The Dutch claimed ownership of parts of the same land by right of the discoveries of Henry Hudson, another explorer in Dutch employ. Generally speaking — al-though there were some exceptions — the English authorities did not pay the Indians for land, because the Crown's opinion was that the "heathens" had no more right to possess "newly found lands" than birds or wild animals.

Dutch patroons like van Rensselaer, Godyn, and others, were expected by the West India Company to give the Indians pres-ents in exchange for deeds covering their patroonships, but the Company itself was very inconsistent. As the reader has seen, the Company paid the Manhattes for Manhattan Island, but at the time of the Swedish expedition, the Dutch had not paid the Indians for land where Fort Nassau was built, nor for Burlington Island where the early Dutch settlement was made, nor for other lands along the Delaware River and its tributaries in New Jersey.

Minuit knew that the Dutch had no Indian deeds for land in the drainage system of the Minquas Kill which he had chosen for Swedish settlement. The only territory the Dutch purchased from the Indians in the present state of Delaware prior to the Swedish expedition, was the land Samuel Godyn's agents bought from the Great Siconese (a Lenape tribe) on June 1,

1629.[11] This property was intended as the Swanendael patroon-ship, and the Indians were paid in trade goods for a strip of land from Cape Henlopen ½ mile wide extending north 32 English miles to the mouth of the South River as discussed in chapter 3. This was in the vicinity of what the English later called Duck Creek, but was then known to the Dutch as Boomtjes, Bomtiens, or Boomptjes Hoeck ("little-tree point"), since corrupted to Bombay Hook.

In his former position as director-general, Minuit had vali-dated this purchase, and he was fully aware that a patent based on the Indian purchase was issued to Godyn on July 11, 1630. Under Dutch law it would be illegal for him to infringe on this purchase. Furthermore, respecting the legality of the Dutch purchase would strengthen his position to buy land from the rightful Indian owners that they had not previously sold to the Dutch. In his judgement his approach to the land problem was legal, honest, and the fair way to deal with the Indian owners. He could not make claim to Swedish explora-tion or prior settlement, as did the Dutch and English, but ownership would be based on a binding contract with the Indian proprietors.

At the sound of cannon blasts from the *Kalmar Nyckel*, the natives were summoned from their camps and villages, and through his Indian interpreter, Andres Lucassen, Minuit sent a message to the Indian leaders to participate with him in negotiating rights to occupy certain land. The deposition made by the four sailors from the *Kalmar Nyckel* then goes on to say:

> The parties were therefore agreed with one another, and thereupon, on the twenty-ninth of March of the above year [1638] appeared and presented themselves before the abovementioned ship's council, in the name of their nations or people, five Sachems or princes, by the name of Mattahorn, Mitot Schemingh [Mitatsemint], Eru Packen [Elupacken], Mahamen, and Chiton . . . . and in the presence of the whole ship's council . . . . ceded, transported, and transferred all

the land, as many days' journeys on all places and parts of the river
[the Minquas Kill] as they [the Swedes] requested; upwards and on
both sides.[12]

The transaction did not occur outdoors on the banks of the
Minquas Kill, nor at one of the native villages, but at a location which had ethnic significance in the Indian culture. Minuit
invited the chiefs or "princes," as they were termed in the
affidavit, to meet with him in the cabin of the *Kalmar Nyckel*.[13]
To the natives this was his home, so to speak, and was a
gesture of sincere hospitality and friendship on his part. Their
acceptance illustrated that they placed their trust in him and
had confidence in his integrity. They evidently did not entertain
any fear that he might order his men to turn their muskets
against them or hold them hostages for tribute from their people.

It seems fitting that this conference should occur on the
vessel that brought the first Swedish expedition to America
by invitation of the man who conceived of the New Sweden
colony. The *Kalmar Nyckel* became the setting where negotiations with the Indians resulted in establishing the first
permanent European settlement in the state of Delaware. The
transaction should not be seen in the context of a routine sale
of land by the Indians in return for swigs of rum and cheap
glass beads. The interpreter took pains to explain the transaction carefully to the sachems because Minuit could not afford
to have any misunderstanding. The documents that were signed
were solemnly executed because Minuit intended the Indian's
consent as the basis for Sweden's claim to land in the Delaware valley. He wanted the land he purchased to be the site of
a major colony which would be occupied not only by Swedes,
but by immigrants from his homeland on the Rhine. Amicable
relations with the local Lenape Indians were absolutely essen-
tial for the future success of New Sweden. The records do not
specifically state what European trade goods were paid to the
Indians, but Minuit was not trying to drive a hard bargain.
He had been instructed to be generous, and there is little ques-

tion there was no haggling over price. The chiefs were given the merchandise they requested, and gifts were also distributed to their followers who were present.

The affidavit of the four sailors leaves no doubt that the ship's council thoroughly understood the significance of the transaction, and the documents bore the signatures of the principal participants acting for the Swedish Crown, as well as two members of the crew who affixed their names as official witnesses.

Unfortunately, the whereabouts of the original deeds signed by the Indian chiefs is not known, nor do we know what happened to the sketch of Fort Christina made by Minuit that accompanied them. These papers were all with the missing log book, and the last records of them was a letter from Blommaert stating he had sent them to Admiral Fleming from Amsterdam.[14] During the centuries that have elapsed they may have been accidentally destroyed in fires, deteriorated from old age, or who knows, they may lie undiscovered in private or institutional collections. The historian lives in hope that such invaluable reference material may some day come to light to corroborate or negate conjectures that must be made.

From a study of the contemporary Swedish and Dutch documents that have survived in which indirect references are made to the Indian purchases of March 29, 1638, Dr. Amandus Johnson surmised that Minuit negotiated two deeds with the Indians. The first transferred land to the Swedes south of the Minquas Kill to Boomtjes Hoeck, or Duck Creek, a distance of approximately 40 miles, and the second from the Minquas Kill north to the Schuylkill River about 27 miles.[15] No western bounds were named because at that time it was not known how far west the land extended. Even though neither of these tracts had been purchased from the Indians by the Dutch, the Dutch were well aware of the territory. They had shown it on their maps, and were responsible for naming some of the geographical features, such as the Minquas Kill. But the West India

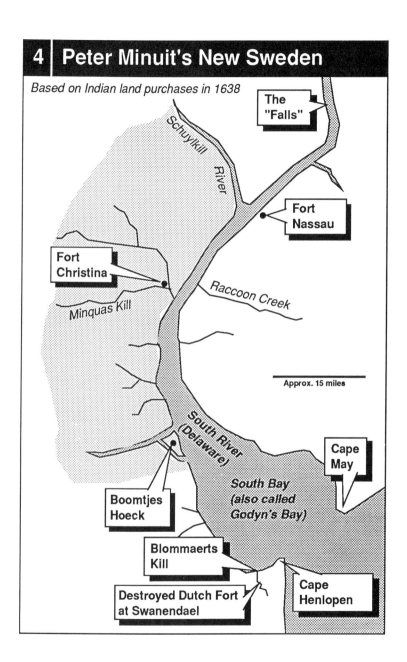

4 | Peter Minuit's New Sweden

Based on Indian land purchases in 1638

The "Falls"

Schuylkill River

Fort Nassau

Fort Christina

Raccoon Creek

Minquas Kill

Approx. 15 miles

South River (Delaware)

Cape May

South Bay (also called Godyn's Bay)

Boomtjes Hoeck

Blommaerts Kill

Destroyed Dutch Fort at Swanendael

Cape Henlopen

Company did not feel it was necessary to negotiate title deeds with the Indians, which they could have done long before. With his knowledge of the terrain, Minuit capitalized on Dutch weakness which must have given him a great deal of personal satisfaction in view of his mistreatment by the West India Company. He also rationalized his occupation by claiming that the land he purchased from the Indians was south of the farthest limits of New Netherland, and even Blommaert was persuaded that the territory Minuit called New Sweden did not belong either to the Dutch or English, but lay between Virginia and New Netherland.[16]

The Lenape Indian concept of land tenure in 1638 differed from Swedish, English, and Dutch traditions of land ownership and sale. That difference must be understood because of later conflicts that developed between Europeans and Indians over the occupation and use of land. Minuit came from a world where all the land belonged to somebody — the government, the church, wealthy landowners like his wife's family, and others. This land was alienable, which simply means one owner could deed outright ownership of his land to another person for a price agreed upon.

This type of permanent individual land ownership did not occur among the Lenape. Land was not possessed in perpetuity in the sense that it permanently belonged to one person or one family. Land use was shared, and legal restraints did not prevent more than one family to use the land, plant on it, hunt animals that lived on it, and build wigwams on it.

Thus, in the deeds which Minuit signed with the Lenape chiefs, he believed in good faith that he had bought outright possession of the land according to European custom. The five Indian chiefs, according to native custom, were under the impression that signing the deeds meant that they were hospitably giving the Swedes the right to share the use of the land with them, but not to transfer permanent ownership to them. The duffel cloth, axes, mirrors, copper pots, and other trade goods that exchanged hands had different meanings to buyers and sellers. The Europeans believed that this merchandise was accepted by the Indians as compensation for permanent possession of the land. The Indians believed that the trade goods were gifts generously tendered to them by the Europeans for the right to share the land with them. But they never intended to relinquish their ancient rights to hunt, fish, and plant on the same land.

Land was vital to native existence; if the Indian dispossessed himself, his family could not survive and that was unheard of. Of course, the Indians could not grasp the nuances in the legal language of the deeds that they signed because of the misunderstanding between Indians and whites over the meanings of the words and phrases. In the years that followed, the Indians quickly learned the European meaning of land sale, and in some instances they specified in the deeds that they retain the rights to hunt, fish, and trap on lands they deeded to white buyers. Nevertheless, it was not easy for them to learn the significance of private ownership, and Indian sellers would appear at intervals after a sale had been made and expect gifts to be given them as a continuing token of the white man's appreciation. This is not an easy subject to understand, and as the years passed there were changes in concepts, misunderstandings, and fraudulent dealings perpetuated by white buyers. Clearly, there was no intent on Minuit's part to defraud the Indians, and land was then so plentiful and cheap that his relations with the Indians were very satisfactory.

After the deeds were signed, the *Kalmar Nyckel* fired a salute of two cannon, and Minuit's soldiers erected the insignia of the Queen of Sweden on poles planted on the shoreline bearing the marks CRS signifying ownership by *Christina Regina Sueciae* (Christina, Queen of Sweden). The men then began erecting the fort which Minuit named Fort Christina in honor of the 12-year-old Swedish queen. The reader may recall that Minuit was instructed to name Sable Island, Christina Island, but inasmuch as he did not go there, the idea of naming the fort after the queen must have been his own.

The only contemporary drawing of Fort Christina known to exist is a ground plan made 16 or 17 years later by the young Swedish engineer Peter Lindeström who accompanied Governor Johan Rising to New Sweden in 1654.[17] By this time a number of additions and modifications had been made in the structure, although the original features can be discerned. It was surrounded by log palisades sharpened at the tops with axes, and set closely together vertically in the form of a square. Four acute-angled bastions, pointed like arrows, projected diagonally from the four corners. Three of them had platforms mounted with cannon taken from the *Kalmar Nyckel*. Except for the northeast side, the site was flanked by tidal marshes that provided natural protection. The main gate swung open on the rocky wharf running down to the landing place in the Minquas Kill where vessels anchored. On the northeast corner of the structure, a back entrance provided access by land via a narrow path that ran into the woods.

Two log houses were erected within the palisaded area, one as a sort of barracks, for men stationed in the fort, and the other as a storehouse for food, supplies, and merchandise intended for the Indian trade. The bricks Minuit brought from Gothenburg were used in the construction of a fireplace, chimney, and oven. The rough benches and tables were probably made of hand-sawed lumber.

The fort was suitable for withstanding an Indian attack, but as a military post to repel European intruders, it was too far up the Minquas Kill to command the Delaware River. Moreover, ships going up and down the river were out of range of the fort's cannon. Minuit was well aware of its military deficiency when he selected the site; his objective was not to control ship traffic in the Delaware, but to avoid a confrontation with the Dutch, yet at the same time block off one of the trade arteries leading to the Minquas country.

Before the fort was completed, Minuit gave orders to Captain Jöransen to take the *Grip* to Jamestown to trade its cargo for Virginia tobacco. This mission occurred after the landing operations were completed in the Minquas Kill, and not while the two vessels were enroute to the Delaware, as stated by some writers. A letter written by Jerome Hawley, treasurer of the Virginia colony, to Sir Francis Windebank in London clarifies the chronology. The letter was dated May 8, 1638, and Hawley stated he had written a progress report to Windebank on March 20, and since that date "heare arrived a Dutch shipp with commission from the young Queene of Sweaden and signed by eight of the Cheife Lordes of Sweaden . . .". He went on to say that the vessel, which we know was the *Grip*, came to obtain tobacco, but Virginia's Governor William Berkeley did not have the authority to enter into free trade with other nationals unless the Crown approved, and he refused to provide Captain Jöransen with any tobacco.

In his letter Hawley reported that the Swedes planned to raise tobacco in the Delaware Bay (although no specific site was named), as the Dutch were already doing in the Hudson River. He recommended that the English government take steps to remove these intruders on lands claimed by England.[18] The *Grip* remained in Jamestown for about 10 days to replenish wood and water and then returned to Fort Christina.

By the time the *Grip* returned, Fort Christina was probably nearing its final stages of construction, and Minuit, Hendrick Huygen, and the boy Gotfried Harmer, who was already showing an aptitude for the Lenape dialect, had already initiated trade with the Indians. Minuit assigned others to till the soil which proved to be very fertile, and corn seed obtained from the Indians was planted along with grains and some vegetables. Wild turkeys, geese, deer, fish, and other edible birds and animals were plentiful, and food was not a problem.

On or about May 20, Minuit sent the *Grip* on an important mission to the Caribbean. Captain Jöransen was instructed to look for vulnerable Spanish vessels which might be carrying silver, gold or sugar, and if he could not find a prize, to load up with salt or any other goods salable in Sweden.[19] The *Grip* was at St. Christopher on June 5 where she took on casks of water and salt, and Jöransen, doubtless at Minuit's instruction, despatched a letter to Blommaert on one of the vessels returning to Holland. He pointed out in the letter that when he left Fort Christina it was Minuit's intention to sail three weeks thereafter in the *Kalmar Nyckel*, stopping enroute in the Caribbean to exchange wines and spirits still in the cargo for tobacco, salt, and other salable commodities, and then return directly home.[20] Upon receipt of the letter Blommaert calculated it was a three week voyage from Fort Christina to St. Christopher, and that Minuit would arrive there about July 7, would remain for about two weeks, and would be back in Sweden three weeks later.[21] This proved to be an overly optimistic surmise, because of circumstances not known to Captain Jöransen.

While the *Grip* was enroute to the Caribbean, Minuit sent the sloop to obtain furs at the Lenape villages on the Schuylkill. He wanted to accumulate as many pelts as possible to take back with him. The sloop was not seen as it passed Fort Nassau, but it was sighted by the garrison as it came downriver. When it sailed upstream a second time, Minuit was personally aboard, and when the vessel reached the fort, the incident was reported to Governor Willem Kieft at New Amsterdam, and in a letter dated April 28, 1638, he wrote the directors in Holland as follows:

> The assistant of Fort Nassau writes that Minuyt was at the South river and had sent his sloop above the fort. He would, afterwards, again go up, which our people prevented. And Peter Mey [assistant commander] sailed down aboard of him, demanding to see his commission which he refused to exhibit, saying he will build a fort there, and his Queen had as much right there as the Company. I have sent Jan Jansen, the Commissary of the fort thither, and instructed him in case Minuyt should attempt anything to our prejudice to protest against him in due form. I hourly expect news from there, etc.[22]

Minuit was not deterred by the Dutch opposition, and on July 31, 1638, Governor Kieft included the following information in a letter to Holland:

> Minuyt erected a fort on the South River five leagues from ours; attracted all of the peltries to himself by means of liberal gifts; departed thence with his two attendant ships, leaving 24 men in the fort provided with all sorts of goods and provisions; he had posts set up with these letters, C.R.S. Jan Jansen, the Commissary at Fort Nassau had protested by my orders, to which he gave an answer, copy whereof is annexed hereunto. [If Minuit replied in writing it has been lost.] We subsequently sent from this place [Fort Amsterdam] a draught of a protest which was read to him, *whereunto he would not answer.*[23]

The italic has been added because it refers to the following message written by Kieft and read to Minuit by Jan Jansen:

> I, William Kieft, Director-General of New-Netherland, residing on the Island of the Manhattes and in Fort Amsterdam, under the authority of their High Mightinesses the Lords States-General of the United Netherlands and the Incorporated West-India Company, Chamber at Amsterdam, make known to you Peter Minuit who style yourself Commander in the service of Her Royal Majesty of Sweden, *that the whole Southriver of New-Netherland has been many years in our possession and secured by us above and below at forts and sealed with our blood, which even happened during your administration of New-Netherland and is well known to you.*
>
> Now, as you intrude between our forts and begin to build a fort there to our disadvantage and prejudice, which shall never be suffered by us and we are very certain, that her Royal Majesty of Sweden has not given you any order to build fortresses on our rivers or along our coasts.
>
> Therefore, in case you proceed with the erection of fortifications and cultivation of the soil and trade in peltries or in any wise attempt to do us injury, We do hereby protest against all damages, expenses and losses, together with all mishaps, bloodsheds and disturbances, which may arise in future time therefrom and that we shall maintain our jurisdiction in such manner, as we shall deem most expedient. [Thus done Thursday, being the 6th May, anno 1638.]

Evidently the document was undated, or the date obliterated, and the words in brackets were supplied by the translator, E. B. O'Callaghan.[24]

Both Swedish ships did not leave at the same time, as one would infer from Kieft's letter of July 31, 1638. The *Grip* left on May 20, as indicated above, and Minuit sailed for St. Christopher about the middle of June, leaving behind 24 men at Fort Christina. Måns Kling was in command of the soldiers, and Hendrick Huygen was in charge of the merchandise and provisions, assisted by Minuit's grandnephew, Gotfried Harmer.

As prearranged by Minuit, the *Grip* returned to Fort Christina early in 1639 having cruised during the winter months in the warm Caribbean waters looking for Spanish prizes. Upon her return to Fort Christina she took aboard pelts purchased after Minuit had departed on the *Kalmar Nyckel*. Due to contrary winds, the *Grip* was unable to leave for home until late April 1639.

Little is known about the exploits of the *Grip*. Somewhere in the Caribbean she took aboard an African slave named Anthony, also spelled Antoni, whose original home was in Angola, the Portuguese colony in West Africa. When the *Grip* sailed from Fort Christina, Anthony was left behind increasing the total population to 25. The *Grip* carried aboard more than 1500 animal pelts which brought a good price for the New Sweden Company as discussed in the next chapter, but no satisfactory report of her gains in the Caribbean were ever entered in the company's records. A rumor persisted that Captain Andrian Jöransen bilked his Swedish employers out of Spanish booty. As late as 1644, Governor Printz lamented that the Dutch supported a privateer that brought four lucrative Spanish prizes to New Amsterdam, and he said that the Swedes could compete aggressively for this wealth if he had a well-fitted ship and a "Swedish captain should be in command to prevent fraud, for when skipper Andrian [Captain Andrian Jöransen, a Dutchman] cruised about here for a few months with the sloop, the *Grip*, it was for his own profit (as his acquaintances . . . . admit and say)."[25]

The *Kalmar Nyckel* and the *Grip* were on their way homeward, and 24 white men and one black man were left behind to hold Fort Christina and protect Swedish interests until reinforcements arrived bringing women and children. How about the six young men employed by Kiliaen van Rensselaer who were paid passengers on the *Kalmar Nyckel*? What happened to them? Despite diligent search not a single reference has been found to them in any of the Swedish records that have been preserved. Only one tantalizing clue appears in a letter Governor Kieft wrote to van Rensselaer from New Amsterdam dated August 14, 1638. It reads as follows:

> Some time ago I sent a shallop up the river expressly with the goods that came with minuyt; now another has gone expressly for you.[26]

This can only mean that Minuit found a way to transport van Rensselaer's passengers and the merchandise in their custody to Manhattan Island. Kieft then used small shallops owned by the Dutch West India Company to complete the delivery of the men and merchandise to Rensselaerswyck. Thus, Peter Minuit faithfully kept a promise he made to an old friend.

Chapter 6 Notes

1. After the return of the *Kalmar Nyckel*, Blommaert obtained the log book which he sent to Admiral Fleming with other papers. Included was a manuscript map apparently made by Minuit, *Blommaert Letters*, No. 35, Nov. 13, 1638.
2. *Blommaert Letters*, No. 33, Jan. 6, 1638.
3. *VRBM*, pp. 393-94.
4. *Ibid.*, p. 396.
5. *Ibid.*, pp. 402-03.
6. *Ibid.*, p. 391.
7. *Ibid.*, p. 395.
8. *Blommaert Letters*, No. 33, Jan. 6, 1638.
9. Minuit's concern about English pretensions to land along the Delaware was well known to Swedes who settled in the colony, see A. R. Dunlap and C. A. Weslager, "More Missing Evidence: Two Depositions By Early Swedish Settlers," *Pennsylvania Magazine of History and Biography* 91 (Jan. 1967): 38.
10. "Affidavit of Four Men From the Key of Calmar," *Narratives, Myers*, pp. 86-89. The above "More Missing Evidence" states that Minuit explored for six weeks and three

days to make certain there was no English or Dutch occupation before going ashore and building Fort Christina, which appears to be an exaggeration, p. 38. It is certainly not corroborated by the *Affidavit*, and the Swedes may have been trying to reinforce Penn's claims to the land.

11. *Weslager, 1961*, pp. 266-69.
12. *Narratives, Myers*, p. 88. The actual phraseology of the *Affidavit* was that the sachems represented the "Ermewormahi . . . the Mante . . . and Minqua nations." The former two are known to have been Lenape bands or subtribes. The Minquas were not residents of the area, but may have been present to ratify the transaction.
13. *Affidavit*, p. 88.
14. *Blommaert Letters*, No. 35, Nov. 13, 1638; No. 36, Jan. 28, 1640. Cf. *SS* 1: n. 30, p. 117.
15. *SS* 1:184. Thirteen years later the chief Mattahorn told the Dutch that the land sold to Minuit was bounded by six trees and was large enough only for a house and a plantation, presumably the site of Fort Christina. His deposition was made to please Governor Peter Stuyvesant who challenged Swedish ownership, and cannot be accepted as unbiased historical evidence. See C. A. Weslager, *The Swedes and Dutch at New Castle* (Wilmington: Middle Atlantic Press, 1987), pp. 63-70.
16. *Blommaert Letters*, No. 36, Jan 28, 1640.
17. The drawing appears as the frontispiece in *SS* 1. Another view appears opp. p. 518 of *SS* 2.
18. *Penna. Archives*, 2nd series, Harrisburg, 1890. 5:59.
19. The departure date of May 20 is given on p. 159 of *Blommaert Letters*, No. 34, Sept. 4, 1638.
20. *Ibid*.
21. *Ibid*. Weather conditions often disrupted these estimates.
22. *NYCD* 1:592.
23. *Ibid*.
24. *NYCD* 12:19. A slightly different version of the letter

from the "Albany Documents" is found in Samuel Hazard, *Annals of Pennsylvania* (Philadelphia: Hazard and Mitchell, 1850), pp. 44-5.

25. Amandus Johnson, *The Instruction For Johan Printz* (Philadelphia: Swedish Colonial Society, 1930): p. 126.

26. *VRBM*, p. 422.

7. A Tragic Return

Måns Kling remained behind at Fort Christina in command of the the garrison consisting of 24 men, mostly Swedes and Dutch, and the Angoler, Anthony — a total of 25. Anthony was the first black man on record in the Delaware River valley, but Minuit never saw him because the Negro arrived on the *Grip* after Minuit's departure on the *Kalmar Nyckel*.

Next to nothing was recorded about Anthony other than the reference to him as "a purchased slave."[1] He was undoubtedly enslaved in West Africa and taken to one of the Caribbean islands, possibly St. Christopher, where Captain Jöransen purchased him. The Swedes did not traffic in slaves, and one can only speculate why Jöransen decided to take him to Fort Christina and leave him there. It is not impossible that Anthony may have worked in the tobacco fields and Jöransen knew that this experience would be valuable to the Swedes who knew nothing about raising the plant. Who knows? Minuit may have asked Jöransen to keep his eyes open for someone who could teach the men in the garrison. The reader will recall that Minuit himself had to hire a Virginia runaway to teach his hired hands at Manhattan to raise tobacco.

However, the men at Fort Christina did not then plant any tobacco, although it was later grown in New Sweden by Swedish and Finnish farmers. Since neither Kling nor Huygen had need for a personal slave, Anthony may have been assigned routine tasks like the other men. Anthony was still in the colony nine years later when his name was included among the "laboring people who are appointed to cut hay for the cattle, and also in the meantime to follow the governor on the little sloop."[2] The governor referred to was Johan Printz who came to New Sweden in 1643, and who had two small sloops at his disposal. The phraseology suggests that Anthony may have been emancipated and allowed to work for wages in the fields and on one of the governor's boats. Regardless of his social position Anthony must be included among the pioneer members of the New Sweden colony even though he did not come from Sweden.

The 24 other men probably volunteered to stay at Fort Christina with Minuit's permission; at least there is no reason to believe that any of them was forced to remain against his will. Even Anthony was probably happy to step on solid earth again, and had no incentive to join the *Grip's* crew for a long voyage to Sweden, a land that he never saw. Possibly he understood, as did the others, that Minuit intended to return with permanent settlers as soon as possible.

The mission of the garrison was to conduct the fur trade, take care of the grains they had planted, and maintain amicable relations with both the Indians and the Dutch. Keeping the Swedish flag flying over Fort Christina was a key objective because everyone understood that it would not be safe for Minuit to return with women and children unless there was a place where the families could be protected against an attack by hostile "wildings," as the Swedes then called the Indians. Converting the Lenape to Christianity was a mission of some of the Swedish pastors later sent to New Sweden, such as Johan Campanius, but there was no preacher in the first expedition. The first contingent had neither the time, inclination, nor training to Christianize the Indians, and self-preservation was their primary interest.

No formal list of the names of the men in Kling's command has been preserved, although it is known that Hendrick Huygen shared executive responsibility in the sense that he maintained under lock and key the supplies, foodstuffs, and the trade goods necessary to assure friendly relations with the Indians. He also carefully guarded the animal pelts which would yield a return to the investors in the New Sweden Company.

Huygen personally traveled to some of the Indian towns to engage in bartering, and his youthful German cousin Gotfried Harmer worked with him as his assistant. Some genealogists believe there may have been French ancestors in Huygen's family tree, but he spoke Dutch fluently and kept account books in well-written Dutch. Some have been carefully preserved.[3] Minuit instructed him and Kling to be more liberal than the Dutch in the amount of merchandise they paid the Indians for furs, which diverted the business from Dutch traders to the Swedes. Governor Kieft complained to his superiors in Amsterdam as early as October 2, 1639 that Swedish competition on the South River was responsible for a substantial decrease in the number of pelts he shipped to Holland.[4]

Probably none of the members of the garrison thought of themselves as brave pioneers who would win fame, or fortune, because they were rooting a new colony. To them they were doing a job they asked for, and were being paid moderate wages for their services, insufficient to make them rich, but more than they could have earned at home. Seen from today's perspective, if courage makes heroes, they all qualified. Living in a strange land with the ever-present danger of wild animals, poisonous snakes, and harassed by mosquitoes and other pesky insects that thrived in the surrounding marshes, did not contribute to their comfort. The account of

how the Indians destroyed the Dutch colony at Swanendael in
the South Bay had then become common knowledge, and distrust of the natives contributed to their anxieties. Kieft, an
Indian hater, didn't let anyone forget that "the mouth of the
river is sealed with our blood." This was especially true when
they left the sloop to hunt deer, wild turkeys, and other edible
animals in the woods where natives hidden behind the trees
could ambush them. Even when they visited the native towns
to buy Indian corn and trade for furs, they knew they were
greatly outnumbered and feared being murdered and their trade
goods stolen.

We understand today that the Lenape were a hospitable
people to visitors who came to their towns with peaceful in-
tentions, but members of the garrison were suspicious and
remained alert for hostility where it did not then exist. No one
in the first expedition ever claimed to have been threatened by
the Indians, and to Minuit's credit the Indians treated his associates with the same respect they had shown towards him.

The approach of winter constituted another danger. We may
be sure that Minuit who had experienced severe winters in
New Netherland, warned both Kling and Huygen to make
certain the men cut plenty of firewood, and split an adequate
supply of logs, to prepare for the possibility of heavy snows.
Huddling around the open fireplace in their crowded barracks
was necessary for survival if they were snowbound during a
long and hard winter. Minuit knew that loneliness would increase during the winter months, and the men would miss their
homes and families; some were married and the fathers of
children, and the unmarried men would grow lonely for parents
or sweethearts.

Despite the miserable loneliness they must have experienced,
they all survived their initial two years of service at Fort Christina while they were cut off from any ties with the homeland.
The barber-surgeon Timen Stiddem, who apparently was one
of the 25, kept the men in good physical condition. Some

contention may have developed as might be expected when
men of differing cultures and national backgrounds are thrown
together, but there is no record of any serious animosities.
This may have been because they all shared one thing in common: the yearning to see the sails of the *Kalmar Nyckel* bearing Swedish colors atop her masts coming into the Minquas
Kill to take them home again.

When Minuit left on the *Kalmar Nyckel* his immediate destination was in Caribbean waters well known to Dutch navigators, and he anticipated no problem in exchanging his cargo
of wines for tobacco. Both he and Captain van der Water
understood the importance of the so-called trade winds that
blow over the seas. Commerce depended upon a knowledge
of these winds to take a sailing vessel to its destination without being stranded in the doldrums because the wind had
calmed. Navigators knew the belts of wind altered with the
seasons, and reaching the destination depended upon these
trade winds whose *course* or *track* (from which the word *trade*
is derived) was normally predictable, provided the pattern was
not disordered by unanticipated storms.

The *Kalmar Nyckel* sailed out of the Minquas Kill about
June 15, 1638 so far as can be determined, and departed from
Delaware Bay on a southerly course.[5] Minuit's instructions
told him, "You shall also run with the ship to the island Seinte
Cristoffer in order somewhere there to trade wine, brandy,
stockings, shoes, etc. (whatever can be spared) for tobacco
seeing to it that the tobacco is not too highly valued, and
getting as much for your merchandise as possible."

The refusal of the English to trade tobacco to the Swedes
on the *Grip's* voyage to Jamestown in May left Minuit no
alternative except to follow his instructions and sail to St.
Christopher. Several decades later he might have obtained fine
quality tobacco on the Eastern Shore of Maryland, but the
young Maryland colony had not yet begun to grow tobacco in
any quantity. Thus, he headed for the Caribbean.

In one of his letters, Blommaert wrote that it took three weeks to reach St. Christopher in the Leeward Islands from Fort Christina, but this may have been a conservative estimate. It was probably not until the third or fourth week in July that the *Kalmar Nyckel* reached this chain of tropical islands south of Puerto Rico where the waters of the Atlantic commingle with those of the Caribbean.

St. Croix, St. Eustatius, St. Barthélemy, St. Martin, and others are among the family of Leeward islets known to vacationists today, but in Minuit's time the best known were St. Christopher, or St. Kitts, Nevis, Antigua, and Montserrat. Of these St. Christopher was the most important commercially even though it is only 68 miles square. Tobacco was its principal product already being exported to England and Holland. The English first settled the island in 1624, but the French soon shared part of the island with English planters and Carib Indians.

The leeward or Caribbean coast of St. Christopher was characterized by fertile soil in the fields that fell away from the foot of the mountains covering the center of the island. Sun and abundant rain contributed to the year-around growing season, and rows of bright green tobacco leaves flourished in these fields curving down to the white beaches. This same side of the island offered a convenient roadstead for sailing vessels, whereas there was then no satisfactory anchorage along the Atlantic or windward coast because of shoals, rugged cliffs, and high seas. White servants and hired help were then employed by the planters to work in the tobacco fields — not blacks. As time passed, the island economy changed radically as sugar canes replaced tobacco, and, as elsewhere in the West Indies, armies of black slaves were imported from Africa to work on the sugar plantations.

Allowing a week or 10 days to discharge her cargo of beverages much in demand, and to load up with tobacco, the *Kalmar Nyckel* must have been ready to sail for home on the trade winds in early August. Exactly where she landed on the island, and the related events are not known due to the absence of the ship's log book or other contemporary accounts. All that is known of the tragic event that occurred is found in the following exerpt from one of Blommaert's letters. This information was reported to him by crew members after the *Kalmar Nyckel's* return to Holland:

> He [Minuit] had there exchanged his cargoes for tobacco, and being ready to depart from there, went with his captain [van der Water] as a guest on board a ship from Rotterdam named *het Vliegende Hert [the Flying Deer]* that lay there and traded. When they were about a half hour from shore, according to the explanation of the officers [from the *Kalmar Nyckel*], the hurricane, an extraordinary storm-wind, which, so men say, comes only once in six or seven years, overtook them, through all the ships. Over twenty were driven seawards from the road, some losing their masts and others perishing, including the ship, the *Flying Deer*, upon which were Minuit and his captain.[6]

The following day the crew of the *Kalmar Nyckel* searched the island waters, but failed to find any clues to the whereabouts of the *Flying Deer*. After several days of further searching and making inquiries of other skippers and sailors, the truth became self-evident. The *Flying Deer* had gone to the bottom in the storm taking with her everyone aboard, including her skipper, and his guests, Peter Minuit and Captain van der Water. Neither the ship nor any of the men aboard her were ever seen again. Then, according to emergency plans Blommaert had made in the event of Minuit's death, the first mate Michel Symonssen took command of the vessel for the return voyage to Sweden.

In reconstructing the tragic events that occurred, it seems reasonable to believe that the captain of the *Flying Deer* may have been acquainted with Minuit, van der Water, or both, and he invited them to come aboard his vessel which lay off the island where they were also anchored. Perhaps he wanted to exchange information and raise glasses socially. This appears to have been a common practice followed by both officers and sailors when they encountered ships flying the flags of their own country in a foreign port. In fact, Blommaert writes in another letter that seven of the sailors from the *Flying Deer* left their ship before the storm to visit another vessel, the *Santa Clara*, at anchor in the harbor. When the hurricane struck, these lucky fellows survived the storm.[7]

During Minuit's and van der Water's visit the hurricanes swept across the island without warning and with such velocity that 20 vessels were torn loose from their moorings and driven out to sea. Even the most experienced sea captain was caught unprepared. Why the *Kalmar Nyckel* and some other vessels like the *Santa Clara* were spared any damage is not explained, but many of the others returned with missing masts after the storm subsided, and some like the *Flying Deer* were forever lost.

So ended the life of the founder of New York City and New Sweden. He never returned to Gothenburg to make a report to Admiral Fleming, nor to command a second expedition to enlarge the colony. With him died his secret ambition to people New Sweden with refugees from the Rhine who had been reduced to poverty by wars in their homeland.

The writer learned from the National Hurricane Center of the U.S. Department of Commerce in Coral Gables, Florida that at the latitude of St. Christopher, hurricanes can be of short duration but very intense. Inasmuch as there was no way to track storms in the 17th century, a hurricane moving at 15 to 20 miles per hour might come as a complete surprise even to experienced mariners. Blommaert's information that hurricanes occurred "once every six or seven years" may be true, because at any given location in the Leeward Islands that is about the average return frequency of a hurricane.

Although there may be no relationship with the West Indies hurricanes, Governor John Winthrop in his *Journal* refers to two noteworthy hurricanes in New England in the fall of 1638.

But of more specific interest, it is a matter of record that the island of St. Christopher experienced a severe tropical storm on August 5, 1638. In what was one of the earliest imprints of a disastrous American weather event, John Taylor reported the occurrence in a London pamphlet of 1638 entitled *Newes and strange Newes from St. Christophers of a tempestuous Spirit, which is called by the Indians a Hurrin-cano or whirle-wind*. The author states that the wind blew men into the air "as if they were no more but ragges, clouts, or feathers," and five ships were lost and 75 men killed.[8]

If this was the same hurricane that swept the *Flying Deer* and other vessels out to sea, which seems probable, it would mean that the hitherto unknown date of Peter Minuit's death can be place on or about August 5, 1638. Certain his commander was dead, Symonssen charted a course on trade winds that brought the *Kalmar Nyckel* to the North Sea in the beginning of October. There she was overtaken by another destructive storm reminiscent of the one that delayed the voyage to America almost a year before. Symonssen ordered the main mast chopped down, an emergency procedure that was not uncommon when upright masts constituted such a hazardous wind barrier that the ship was in danger of blowing over.[9] Suffering other storm damages, the *Kalmar Nyckel* managed to reach Vlieland in the West Frisian Islands off the Dutch coast. When the storm subsided, repairs were made at a cost of 7,103:2 florins which was charged to Samuel Blommaert. He promptly sent copies of the bills to Spiring and Fleming requesting that the Swedes remit their share of the expense. The *Kalmar Nyckel* then proceeded to Medemblik where Symonssen had been instructed to unload the peltries, and then proceed to Sweden with the tobacco.

After docking in Medemblik in late October, the *Kalmar Nyckel* ran into another problem with representatives of the West India Company who had her placed under arrest over the question of paying import duties, and whether or not her commander was in possession of suitable master's papers to validate his commission. Messages were sent to Baron Spiring at the Hague for assistance, and he protested to the States General. The issue was finally straightened out after a delay lasting about two months.[10]

The *Kalmar Nyckel* did not get back to Gothenburg until early in 1639. She had been gone 15 or 16 months, after having survived two major ocean storms and a destructive Caribbean hurricane. Minuit was not proudly standing on the deck to bring her into the harbor, but his memory lived on in the hearts of the crew, and the sound of his voice still echoed in their ears. When a man loved a ship, as he did, even death cannot readily separate them.

While she was in Medemblik, the *Kalmar Nyckel* unloaded the following pelts which were then sold in the market for the benefit of the Dutch investors:

511 beaver skins	4,505 florins	
157 otter skins	700 florins	
42 bear skins	712 florins	
710	5,917 florins	

The *Grip*, which arrived back to Gothenburg about the middle of June (without going to Holland) brought back the following pelts which were reshipped to Holland and sold there. There was a bigger demand for pelts in Holland than in Sweden and they brought a better price there than in Gothenburg:

1,258 beaver skins	7,860.12 florins	
157 otter skins	605 florins	
90 bear skins	882 florins	
other skins	162:1:8 florins	
1,505 +	9,509:13:8 florins	

The total amounted to 15,426:13:8 florins.[11] However, this did not include the tobacco brought back by the two vessels, which was sold in Sweden for a total of 18,649 florins. Thus, the total income from the first voyage amounted to 34,075 florins. The wages, supplies, and goods for the Indian trade amounted to more than 46,000 florins. The expedition was plainly not self-supporting. The Swedish investors were not discouraged because they believed they were investing in the future and had made a very promising beginning.

The Swedes appeared to understand that the unforeseen delays in launching the expedition, and the loss of time and cost of repairs resulting from storms, were largely responsible for depressing the income. The impatient Dutch sponsors, including Blommaert, didn't seem able to reconcile themselves to these unbudgeted expenses, and they were disappointed in the unsatisfactory financial yield of the expedition. They based their expectations on comparisons with the performance of the West India Company which enjoyed a substantially larger business in both furs and tobacco. They lost sight of the fact that the West India Company was then in business for more than 15 years, and this was the New Sweden Company's first commercial venture.

The important result of the expedition was that it convinced the Swedish sponsors that Minuit had correctly assessed the opportunities existing for Sweden in the American market. All the furs they imported could be sold in the Netherlands, and elsewhere, at a good profit, and the market for tobacco in Sweden, still in its infancy, was increasing by leaps and bounds. Furthermore, both Oxenstierna and Admiral Fleming now fully understood that transplanting Swedish culture to the New World was an objective to be desired, as Minuit maintained from the beginning.

Chapter 7 Notes

1. *SS* 2:710.
2. *Ibid.*, p. 706.
3. *SS* 1:n.125, p. 336.
4. *NYCD* 1:592.
5. *SS* 1:117.
6. This information is found in the *Blommaert Letters*, No. 35, Nov. 13, 1638, and No. 36, Jan. 28, 1640. The English translation was made by the late Dr. A. R. Dunlap, and first published in *Weslager, 1961*, pp. 182-83. An inaccurate statement was published by the Swedish pastor Israel Acrelius in 1759 to the effect that Minuit died at Fort Christina, *A History of New Sweden*, trans. William M. Reynolds, (Philadelphia: Historical Society of Pennsylvania Memoirs, 1874) v. 11, p. 28. Acrelius's error was perpetuated by a number of later historians, such as Samuel Hazard, *Annals of Pennsylvania* (Philadelphia: Hazard and Mitchell, 1850). p. 59.
7. *Blommaert Letters*, No. 35, Nov. 13, 1638.
8. Information in a personal letter from Gilbert B. Clark, Hurricane Specialist at Coral Gables, dated January 16,

1989. After the writer received this information, Ms. Peggy Tatnall brought to his attention an excellent historical study of the West Indies, Richard S. Dunn, *Sugar and Slaves* (New York: W.W. Norton & Co., 1973). In discussing the Leeward Islands, Dr. Dunn cites the same London pamphlet of 1638 and comments on other hurricanes that subsequently damaged St. Christopher in the seventeenth century, pp. 42-43.

9. *Blommaert Letters*, No. 35, Nov. 13, 1638; *ibid.*, No. 36, Jan. 28, 1640.
10. *NYCD* 1:116-17.
11. *SS* 1:119.

8. *Kalmar Nyckel's* Three Later Voyages

New Sweden was in existence under Swedish control from 1638 to 1655 when the territory was seized by the Dutch. During those 17 years there were 12 expeditions to the colony in which the following ships participated: *Kalmar Nyckel, Fogel Grip, Freedenburgh, Charitas, Swan, Fama, Gyllene Haj (Golden Shark), Katt (Cat), Örn (Eagle),* and the *Mercurius.* The *Swan, Fama,* and *Haj* each made two voyages, and all the others made only one, except the *Kalmar Nyckel* which made *four.* The first voyage of 1638 is the one for which she is best known, but the others briefly discussed below, all made important contributions to the New Sweden colony.

Second Voyage 1639-1640

Even before the *Kalmar Nyckel* returned to Sweden from the first voyage, Admiral Fleming began laying plans for a second expedition with the objective of sending a number of vessels with colonists and supplies. The development of a Swedish colony in the New World, was uppermost in his planning, and Chancellor Oxenstierna fully concurred. This was a bone of contention with the Dutch investors in the New Sweden Company whose principal interest was in making the maximum profits on their investments, not in contributing to

Swedish colonial expansion. Fleming was sorrowed when he received the news of Minuit's untimely death from Spiring, because Minuit, who had first aroused Fleming's interest in establishing *"Nova Sweediae"* was his choice to command a second expedition.

When the deeds, documents, drawings, and maps originating with Minuit reached Fleming from Holland, after the arrival of the *Kalmar Nyckel* at Medemblik, it was as though Minuit was personally urging him to disregard the Dutch opposition. But finances were an important consideration, and after the *Kalmar Nyckel* arrived in Gothenburg, Blommaert and the other Dutch investors threatened to withhold all financial support. A contributing factor was the added expense of paying the crew and officers of the *Grip* when they returned to Gothenburg. Captain Jöransen had brought back no Spanish gold, silver, or sugar, as Blommaert expected, and new cash was needed to compensate him and his men.

If Fleming had given any thought to including the *Grip* as a hunter in the second expedition, that idea had to be forgotten. While the *Grip* lay at anchor at Gothenburg a severe storm in August of 1639 drove her on sandshoals despite the two anchors mooring her. Her cannon and ballast were salvaged, but she would not float, and apparently was left to founder.[1]

After some discussion with the Dutch, prolonged by the fact that messages had to pass back and forth between Stockholm and Holland, it was decided that the *Kalmar Nyckel* would return alone under the command of Cornelis van Vliet, a Dutch skipper in Swedish service, with Herman Willemsen as mate. That fell short of Fleming's expectations, but it was better than nothing since Fleming knew that the garrison of 24 Swedes and Dutch at Fort Christina were awaiting relief. Captain van Vliet was instructed to work closely with Blommaert in Amsterdam where sailors were hired and supplies purchased, according to the pattern set in the first expedition. Van Vliet's charge was to command the vessel — not to remain in the colony as the director, which would have been Minuit's assignment if he had lived. To van Vliet the *Kalmar Nyckel* was merely one of many vessels he had commanded; he bore her no love as Minuit did, and a voyage to New Sweden was just another job. His main interest was in the pay, not in the colony.

Locating a successor to Minuit to remain in the colony as a governor proved to be very difficult. There was a dearth of men with suitable experience, and those Swedes who might have qualified were not interested in the job. Fleming asked Baron Spiring in Holland to find a suitable candidate there, which he tried to do. He finally wrote Fleming that "he knew of no one whom he could recommend" which left the choice to Fleming. As a Finn and a navy officer he made the kind of selection one would expect. His choice was Peter Hollender Ridder who held a commission as a lieutenant in the admiralty. He was born about 1607 in Finland, son of a Dutch merchant who became a customs officer there. His mother Anna Roberts-dotter may have been Finnish, and Ridder, who spoke fluent Dutch, was probably also conversant in Finnish.[2]

Finding volunteers in Sweden to go to America as colonists was a more difficult task than Fleming realized. What was needed, he wrote to Chancellor Oxenstierna on July 1, 1639, were artisans such as blacksmiths, shoemakers, carpenters, bricklayers, and others, three or four of whom should be married and take their wives along to cook, make beer, and wash for the people.[3] He seemed to be thinking of a communal society where a small number of industrious females provided certain domestic service to everyone. Needless to say, this was not a motivator to attract Swedish women to leave their homeland and settle in the American wilderness.

In the search for potential settlers the governor of Gothenburg was asked for his assistance, but he was unable to find any volunteers. However, he made a suggestion that proved to be acceptable to the Crown; occasionally soldiers would desert the army and flee to their own homes. As a new form of punishment for this infraction of military discipline, and for other soldiers who had committed minor misdemeanors, he recommended that they should be sent to America with their families.[4]

The governor of Gothenburg and two other governors, were instructed to find such candidates, and send them to Gothenburg to be in readiness for departure. In addition to the suit of clothes furnished by the government, each was to be given ten daler in copper money. They were not sentenced to permanent banishment, but were allowed to return in one or two years, if they so desired. Of course, not everyone who joined the Ridder expedition was a deserter; a number of respected officers and law-abiding farm folk decided to go along as preparations for the *Kalmar Nyckel's* departure were being made. The original intention was to send a large number of horses and cattle, but only four mares and two young horses accompanied the expedition.

Only one brief letter of instructions issued to Ridder has been located to date. The following English translation by Dr. Richard H. Hulan is published in full for the first time:[5]

> Whereas he has been received and commissioned in our most gracious Queen's service, as Commandant of Fort Christina in New Sweden, to have oversight of the people garrisoned there now and yet to be sent over:
>
> He shall therefore be obliged to seek with all his might Her Most August Majesty's advantage and benefit, and the Participants' profit; to help, to his utmost capacity, to hinder and ward off their injuries and wants; and so to conduct himself in everything that he multiplies it, and the said Most August Majesty and every honest man can and may confidently answer for it, otherwise [to conduct] himself in the rest according to the Special Instruction Captain Cornelius Van Vliet is going to leave upon his departure from there.[6]
>
> It is therefore ordered that the people in the said Fort show him all cooperation and obedience in that which he shall with the advice of the Commissary [Joost van Langdonk], ask and command them.
>
> Done at Stockholm July 1, 1639
> Claes Flemingh

The reader has seen that women and children were absent on the *Kalmar Nyckel's* first voyage in 1638. The men left in the garrison were intended to protect the site selected by Minuit until he returned with colonists. The *Kalmar Nyckel's* second voyage of 1639-1640 with regard to settlers may be compared with the *Mayflower's* voyage which brought the Pilgrims to the shores of Plymouth Bay in 1620, but there were important differences. The names of the passengers on the *Mayflower* are known, but no passenger list was compiled for those on the *Kalmar Nyckel*. Nevertheless, by a careful analysis of a roll of settlers known to be living in New Sweden in 1648, supplemented by a military payroll compiled during Governor Printz's administration, and a synthesis of names found in other sources, Peter S. Craig, the leading authority on the demography of New Sweden, has compiled a list of some of the passengers which he believes arrived on the second voyage. This tabulation, which is given in the *Appendix*, is not purported to be exhaustive, but it is the first list that anyone has attempted to compile. Future historical research may necessitate amendments, but it is the best that can now be supported by the documentation.

The *Mayflower* brought Separatists who came from England to avoid religious persecution. The passengers on the *Kalmar Nyckel* had no religious motives because they enjoyed relative religious freedom in Sweden. The *Mayflower's* destination was Virginia, but it mistakenly landed in Massachusetts where the Pilgrims had no charter or land ownership rights. Conversely, the *Kalmar Nyckel* brought settlers to a predetermined location already purchased by Peter Minuit from the Indian owners.

In making comparisons with the *Mayflower*, it might be noted that two babies were born on her voyage to America, a boy named Perigriene and a girl named Oceanus.[7] A baby was also born on the *Kalmar Nyckel's* second voyage, a son Olof (Olle) born to Sven Gunnarsson and his wife. See *Appen-*

dix. The sons took the patronym Svensson which was Americanized to the surname Swanson, and the family became important landowners.

Misfortune struck the *Kalmar Nyckel* after she sailed from Gothenburg in the beginning of September in 1639 with "people, horses, fodder, and provisions."[8] The vessel sprang a leak in the North Sea which made it too risky to proceed into the Atlantic, and Captain van Vliet sailed to Medemblik to have repairs made. After the leaks were caulked, he took the ship to sea again, but the leaks reappeared, and he again turned back to Medemblik. Baron Spiring was informed at the Hague of the delay, and he notified Blommaert, and both of them went to Medemblik concerned about the unanticipated expenses. There part of the cargo was unloaded and two master carpenters employed to make the needed repairs. They found that the wooden nails, or pegs, below the water line had rotted, and replacements were made. During this waiting period the crew, passengers, and livestock were consuming food, and the crew was running up extra time.

The ship again left the harbor when the work was completed, but when she arrived at Texel she was leaking again, and Captain van Vliet brought her to Amsterdam where it was learned the carpenters hired at Medemblik had not done a satisfactory job.[9] The tarred oakum and cotton wicking driven into the seams between the planks did not make a satisfactory seal.

Spiring and Blommaert were called again. They found that not only had the captain been derelict in supervising the work, but when they checked the cargo, they found that van Vliet had submitted a bill for two barrels of butter and two barrels of herring which were missing. Furthermore, he reported buying 38 barrels of beer at Medemblik, but there were only 31 in the cargo.[10] Other goods were missing, and it was apparent the captain was cheating the company. Baron Spiring accused him of fraud and removed him from office. A new captain, Powel (Pauwel) Jansen, was engaged to command the ship, and several new sailors had to be hired to replace those who quit their jobs probably because they were disgusted with what had happened. The new hands, however, wouldn't go aboard ship unless they were paid two months wages in advance.

When the ship was finally ready to sail again, a major storm swept the Dutch coast beginning on December 27, and this delayed all shipping for some time. It was almost a repetition of the *Kalmar Nyckel's* first voyage, except instead of leaving on December 31, she did not weigh anchor until February 7, 1640. The emergency expenses far exceeded the estimated costs of the voyage, and so far as the Dutch investors were concerned this was the straw that broke the camel's back.

The circumstances all led up to the Swedish government releasing Dutch participation in the New Sweden Company in the autumn of 1641. All of the Dutch investors, including Blommaert, were paid a sum agreed upon. Thereafter, the company was reorganized and operated under Swedish capital.[11] For a while thereafter, although he was no longer an investor, Blommaert continued to retain his position as a Swedish representative in Amsterdam.

In the meantime, as the *Kalmar Nyckel* began its second transatlantic voyage, the officers started to quarrel with each other. Joost van Langdonk, who had been hired as the commissary to replace Hendrick Huygen at Fort Christina, did not get along with Gregorius van Dyck, a competent Dutchman who was pro-Swedish and went along as his assistant. Ridder also had differences of opinion with van Langdonk, which were worsened by the excessive drinking of both van Langdonk and Captain Jansen. Some of the sailors were unruly and also drank to excess from the barrels of beer in the hold. The Reverend Reorus Torkillus, one of the passengers, and the first Lutheran minister to be sent to the colony, was harassed by the captain and those crew members who were Calvinists and prejudiced against Lutherans. Discipline aboard ship was lacking, and the rough voyage across the Atlantic caused many of the passengers to become seasick.[12]

Despite the adversity the *Kalmar Nyckel* arrived at "the Rocks" in the Minquas Kill on April 17, 1640 where crew and passengers were enthusiastically greeted by Måns Kling, Huygen, and the other men. The passengers were as happy to step on dry land again after a distressing voyage as the men in the garrison were to see women and children, and to receive the latest news. Unless an account of Minuit's death had reached them indirectly through the Dutch, it was their first news of the tragedy. Hendrick Huygen must have grieved to learn of the death of his uncle because of the deep affection they had felt for each other.

Ridder did not then realize until he had further discussions with Kling that his arrival with supplies and reinforcements came none too soon, because Kling and the men at the fort were on the verge of abandoning the settlement. They never expected that almost two years would elapse without a relief ship arriving from Sweden. Governor Kieft, or some of his associates, may have persuaded Kling and his men that the government of Sweden had deserted them. Kieft wrote a letter to Amsterdam in which he said he offered the Swedes temporary haven in the Dutch settlement on Manhattan Island. He indicated he had made an agreement with them that if no assistance arrived within two months from April 4, 1640 he would arrange to transport them to Holland on ships of the West India Company.[13] Since Ridder arrived on April 17, well within this grace period, there was no necessity for the men to vacate Fort Christina.

Dutch records confirm that Governor Kieft wrote to Holland on May 31, 1640 stating, "The Swedes on the South River were resolved to move off and come here. On the day before their departure a ship arrived with reinforcements . . ."[14]

He repeated this in a second letter dated October 15, 1640 in which he said, "The Swedes on the South River were last spring reinforced with a ship [the *Kalmar Nyckel*], and fresh settlers and goods. Otherwise they were entirely agreed to come over here with our people &c."[15]

Both letters were addressed to the "Managers of the Incorporated West India Company at Amsterdam," and it is unlikely that Kieft would have directly reported a falsehood to the top management.[16] If we accept his statements at face value it means that the timely arrival of the *Kalmar Nyckel* on her second voyage preserved the colony.

The second voyage of the *Kalmar Nyckel* was also indirectly responsible for contributions to the colony made by Ridder. He extended the bounds of New Sweden by purchasing lands from the Indians on the west bank of the Delaware from the Schuylkill to the falls of the river opposite present Trenton; also the territory from Duck Creek south to Cape Henlopen. He also purchased lands from the Indians on the east side of the river from the Narraticons or present Raccoon Creek southward to Cape May. This was the first Swedish purchase of land in New Jersey.[17] See Map No. 5. Governors Printz and Rising later enlarged the colony by additional land purchases from the Indians shown on later maps.

Ridder moved the two log houses Minuit built in Fort Christina to the east side, and then erected three additional dwellings and a stable. The first church service in New Sweden conducted by an ordained minister was held by the Reverend Torkillus in one of the buildings in the fort. Whether or not a regular chapel was built is not recorded, but Elizabeth Montgomery, who wrote 138 years ago when memories of the early Swedes were fresher than today, said that the Swedes built a chapel *within* the fort, but this may be part of local lore.[18]

Further details of events that occurred in the colony under Ridder's administration are told in other sources which interested readers may want to consult.[19] The author's present focus is on the *Kalmar Nyckel* which left the colony on May 14, 1640 with a large cargo of furs. Måns Kling, Hendrick Huygen, and most of the others in the original garrison returned home on the vessel. The total population of New Sweden in 1640 after the *Kalmar Nyckel* left was probably less

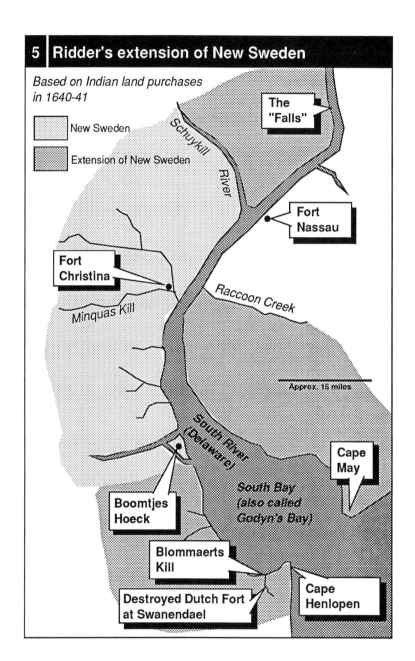

5 | Ridder's extension of New Sweden

Based on Indian land purchases in 1640-41

New Sweden

Extension of New Sweden

The "Falls"

Fort Nassau

Schuykill River

Fort Christina

Minquas Kill

Raccoon Creek

Approx. 15 miles

South River (Delaware)

South Bay (also called Godyn's Bay)

Cape May

Boomtjes Hoeck

Blommaerts Kill

Destroyed Dutch Fort at Swanendael

Cape Henlopen

than 50 men, women, and children. Had Minuit lived to bring farmers from the Rhineland on the second voyage, as he planned, the population would certainly have been larger.[20]

Third Voyage 1641-1642

On her third voyage to New Sweden the *Kalmar Nyckel*, still on loan to the company by the government, was accompanied by a large freight vessel known as a flojt or flöt named the *Charitas (Charity)*. The *Kalmar Nyckel* was commanded by a Dutchman named Andrian Jansen from Saardam, and her first mate was Lambert Pietersen. Her crew consisted of about 32 men with Swedes and Finns predominating although there were also Dutch members. The crew included a chief gunner, carpenter, sailmaker, barber, cook, boatswain, steward, waiter, and a number of musketeers as well as soldiers. The voyage was supported entirely by Swedish finances, and the Swedish government took a more active interest in the expedition as a co-sponsor with the company. Both Chancellor Oxenstierna and Admiral Fleming were determined to support Peter Hollender Ridder with new settlers and supplies because the expansion of the Swedish empire was uppermost in their thoughts.

The *Charitas* was outfitted at Stockholm where animals and passengers, as well as supplies, were taken aboard. The *Kalmar Nyckel* was made ready for the voyage at Gothenburg, her home base, and she also took on passengers and supplies there.

On May 3, 1641, the *Charitas* left Stockholm for the 10 day trip to Gothenburg. With a crew of about 25 officers and men she had 35 passengers aboard, and fortunately their names were all recorded.[21] When the *Charitas* arrived at Gothenburg, an unknown number of these passengers were transferred to the *Kalmar Nyckel* to allow more space on the *Charitas* for additional supplies, livestock, and hay and oats. The vessels left Gothenburg together in July of 1641, but no complete list exists of the passengers. It is known that Måns Kling with his wife and child, and Hendrick Huygen were aboard ship having decided to return to the colony. Huygen was engaged to resume his position as commissary, and Kling was promoted to a lieutenant. Both men, at the request of the government, had been hard at work encouraging people to migrate to New Sweden by touting the beauty of the land and the wonderful opportunities existing there.

Among the settlers on the expedition were a considerable number of Finns then living in the country areas of Sweden where they or their ancestors had migrated from Finland. Because there were insufficient Swedish volunteers, the government met the need for settlers by deporting some of these Finns. The reason given for their deportation was that they had disobeyed Swedish laws by burning down valuable trees to make farmland, or had infracted hunting laws by shooting elks for their hides and then allowing the animals' bodies to lie in the woods and rot. Those who were arbitrarily classified as vagrants were also deported.[22]

The deported Finns were then known by Swedish names, and separating Swedes from Finns cannot be done solely on the basis of family names. Through a careful analysis of a number of documentary sources, starting with the 35 persons who boarded the *Charitas* in Stockholm, and using the aforementioned roll list of settlers known to have been in Sweden in 1648, Peter S. Craig has compiled a list of the passengers in the 1641 expedition which is also given in the *Appendix*. The reader should keep in mind that there were two ships in the expedition, and unless a specific reference was made to one or more of the passengers, there is no certain way of knowing which were on the *Charitas* and which were on the *Kalmar Nyckel*. The list is not exhaustive, and there were many settlers whose date and mode of entry to New Sweden was never recorded. The list is the best that can be offered at present, and is subject to revision when and if new data come to light.

The two vessels arrived at Fort Christina on November 7, 1641, and Ridder was happy to receive the foodstuffs, bags of seeds, tools, building supplies, merchandise for the Indian trade, and especially the farm animals. Some had died during the voyage, but five horses, eight cows, five sheep, and two goats were landed alive. The new colonists also provided some of the skills badly needed in the colony. Ridder was glad to have Lieutenant Kling to reorganize and strengthen the garrison with soldiers who had accompanied him. He was especially relieved to have Hendrick Huygen replace van Langdonk, because of the former's experience in the first expedition, and one who had the respect of Swedes and Dutch alike.

Thoughts of Peter Minuit and recollections of the first voyage of the *Kalmar Nyckel* must have been on Huygen's mind during the voyage, because he knew how dedicated his uncle had been in his ambition to establish the New Sweden colony. Who can say that Huygen's determination to return and contribute to the growth of the colony was not partially due, at least, to the deep affection he felt for his deceased uncle? Can there be any doubt that he could feel Minuit's presence on the *Kalmar Nyckel* as the vessel anchored at "the Rocks?"

The two ships took their departure from Fort Christina about November 29, 1641, although their cargoes were very light since English traders from Connecticut ruined the fur trade after Ridder's arrival.[23] No exportable tobacco was yet raised in New Sweden, although a small quantity had been obtained from Virginia, but not enough for a full cargo. The *Kalmar Nyckel* and *Charitas* set a course for Rochelle in France where quantities of salt were taken aboard both vessels, but not nearly enough to pay for the expensive voyage.[24] In fact, the company had to borrow 3000 R.D. at 10% interest to meet the expenses which included the salaries of the ships' companies, and the accumulated pay of the men they brought back with them from the colony.[25]

About April 15, 1642, the two ships returned to Gothenburg. In the summer or fall of the same year, Samuel Blommaert resigned his position as the Swedish agent in Amsterdam, probably because of mounting pressures among his Dutch confreres to his Swedish association which had the appearance of betraying his countrymen. Although his duties were taken over by Swedish diplomats, both the New Sweden Company and the Crown lost the talents of an irreplaceable promoter who with Minuit and Baron Spiring deserve the credit of awakening interest in Sweden in sponsoring a colony in the New World.

Fourth Voyage 1643-1645

The fourth and last voyage of the *Kalmar Nyckel* in New World waters took place in the company of another armed vessel called the *Fama (Fame)*. The *Fama* had recently returned with the *Swan* from New Sweden after transporting the Johan Printz expedition. Printz relieved Ridder on February 15, 1643, and succeeded him as governor. Having newly arrived in Gothenburg, the *Fama* had to be overhauled and made ready for a new voyage. On the outward voyage she ran ashore in a snowstorm in Delaware Bay and suffered considerable damage.[26] Emergency repairs were made at Fort Christina, but she had to be made shipshape at Gothenburg before setting sail again. The punishment to which these vessels were exposed is difficult to imagine — wind, rain, blistering sunshine, corrosive salt spray, and battering waves in normal service were made worse by mishap and storm damage, all of which contributed to their deterioration. For each there would come a day of reckoning when they could no longer be patched or repaired, and they left for a voyage from which they did not return, or they were decommissioned and sold to the highest bidder for disposition.

The cargo loaded aboard the *Fama* consisted of specific supplies Printz had requested be shipped to him — farming and building tools, clothing, shoes, bricks, lime, and pitch, as well as a preponderance of Indian trade goods to enable him to engage in business on a grand scale with the Indians. In this instance the names of her crew have been preserved as well as those of nine passengers who intended to remain in the colony; her skipper was Peter Paulsson, a Dutchman from Edam.[27]

The *Kalmar Nyckel*, having been made seaworthy from the wear and tear of her recent voyages, was loaded with merchandise to be exchanged in the Caribbean for tobacco. Included were a large quantity of wooden spoons, wooden bottles, wooden basins, lumber and tar obtained in Sweden, and brandy, wine, and beer purchased in Holland.[28]

Captain Berent Hermansson Hopp was placed in command, and he initially made a list of the 41 crew members with the caption "Crew list of the *Kalmar Nyckel commissioned to the West Indies 1643.*"[29] No passengers' names were shown on this list and perhaps none were then intended to accompany him. Changes occurred that revised the roster, and after his return from the voyage, Captain Hopp made a second listing on June 15, 1645 with the caption "Register of all the souls *transported aboard the ship Kalmar Nyckel to New Sweden.*" The ship's company on this roster numbered 37 pesons, and, in addition, two passengers "who are going to stay in the country." Their names were listed as "John Papegoja from Rarstorp [sic] and Walle Liur from Jönköping." As we know, these men were Johan Papegoja, a young aristocrat from Ramstorp who was destined to become an officer in the colony and to marry Governor Printz's eldest daughter Armegot; and Walle Liur (Looe, Looer, Lohe) recruited by Papegoja to serve as a soldier in New Sweden.

Most historians, including the writer, have accepted Amandus Johnson's interpretation that after the two ships left Gothenburg on December 29, 1643, they traveled together to American waters and there separated, the *Kalmar Nyckel* sailing to St. Christopher and the *Fama* continuing alone to Fort Christina.[30] The Swedish historian Alf Åberg recently pointed out that Johnson was not aware of the existence of the crews and passenger lists compiled by Captain Hopp indicating the

Kalmar Nyckel brought two passengers to New Sweden. This, and other data, lead one to agree that both ships went to New Sweden, and after delivering her passengers, the *Kalmar Nyckel* went to St. Christopher.[31]

A letter written by Papegoja to Count Per Brahe after his arrival in New Sweden states that the voyage lasted two months, and "the 27th of February [1644] we caught sight of Virginia and came safely ashore and found the Governor [Printz] and our own in good health . . ."[32] Papegoja was doubtless using the term Virginia to apply to the North American mainland, probably the mouth of Delaware Bay.

Governor Printz stated specifically in his first report that, "The ship *Fama* arrived here in New Sweden on the 11th of March, and is sent away in the name of God on the 11th of June."[33] Since Captain Hopp's records indicate Papegoja was a passenger on the *Kalmar Nyckel*, the latter must have preceded the *Fama* to New Sweden, and after her two passengers debarked, continued on to the Caribbean. The records show she was in St. Christopher on May 5 where Captain Hopp bought a quantity of tobacco.[34] After unloading her cargo, and putting the tobacco aboard, he may have waited for the *Fama* by pre-arrangement so they could return home together. Both captains must have been aware that the war between Sweden and Denmark had broken out, and it was safer for two ships carrying valuable cargoes to travel together, their combined gun power giving them added protection.

The next information on record about the two vessels is found in the Dutch archives where notice was recorded of their arrival in Holland. The *Fama* arrived first, sometime prior to October 8, 1644, anchoring at Harlingen, and the *Kalmar Nyckel*, which had stopped in Dover for needed supplies, arrived some weeks later, date not recorded.[35]

The cargo delivered by the *Fama* consisted of 2,137 whole or partial beaver pelts, and 22,019 pounds of leaf tobacco, whereas the *Kalmar Nyckel* carried 70,421 pounds of tobacco.[36]

Both ships were held by Dutch customs for the payment of import duty to the government and an 8% toll to the West India Company before discharging their cargoes. If Samuel Blommaert were still representing Sweden in Amsterdam he could have blocked this bureaucratic interference, but he lived for only two years after leaving Swedish service in 1642.

Because of disputes over these charges which delayed unloading the goods, Baron Spiring at the Hague was forced to intervene through diplomatic channels on behalf of the Swedish government. His protests resulted in the States General on April 21, 1645 ordering that "the cargo of the Royal ships the *Calmer sleutel* and *Fama coming from Nova Swecia, a district in the possession of her Royal Majesty* . . . may be discharged without making any further difference therein."[37] Since the island of St. Christopher was not part of the territory in Swedish possession, the writer interprets this as further evidence that the *Kalmar Nyckel* was, in fact, in New Sweden on her voyage. It is unlikely that Spiring, an agent of the Swedish Crown dealing with top level Dutch officials, would have made this statement in important diplomatic correspondence if the facts did not support it.

Chapter 8 Notes

1. *SS* 1:n. 28, p. 125; *SS* 2:n. 7, p. 758.
2. Olavi Koivukangas, "The Beginning of Finnish Migration to the New World," *Exhibition Catalog*, Institute of Migration, Turku, Finland, 1988, p. 78. Cf. Karl Gustav Olin, *Våra första Amerika farare* Jakobstad, Finland, 1988, p. 14.
3. *SS* 1:125-26. Women's tasks in New Sweden were not easy ones. When Governor Johan Rising, a bachelor, wrote Eric Oxenstierna to send him a good wife, he said women's labors are "to look after the garden and the cattle, to spin and to weave both the linen and the wool with which to clothe the people, to keep the nets and seines in order, to make malt, to brew the ale, to bake, to cook the food, to milk the cows, to make the cheese and butter." *SS* 2:545-46. He neglected to add that bearing the children and raising the children was also a prime responsibility.
4. *SS* 1:126.
5. The Swedish National Archives, Stockholm, kindly supplied a photocopy of the document. There must have been other instructions requiring Ridder not to begin hostilities with the Dutch, *SS* 1:200.

6. Van Vliet was authorized to give further written instructions to Ridder after he, van Vliet, sized up the situation at Fort Christina. However, van Vliet never reached the colony as discussed above.
7. *William Bradford's History "Of Plimoth Plantation"* (Boston: Wright and Potter Printing Co., 1899).
8. *Blommaert Letters, No. 36, Jan. 28, 1640, p. 532.*
9. *Ibid.*
10. *SS* 1:128.
11. *Ibid.*, p. 132.
12. *Ibid.*, pp. 129-30.
13. *Ibid.*, pp. 142-43.
14. *NYCD* 1:593.
15. *Ibid.*
16. Johnson's assumption that the Swedish garrison never intended to desert Fort Christina because neither Ridder nor Van Dyck mentioned it in letters they wrote to Fleming and Oxenstierna, is a tenuous argument in view of Kieft's statement, *SS* 1:196. Neither of them had access to Kieft's letters quoted above.
17. *SS* 1:201-02.
18. Elizabeth Montgomery, *Reminiscences of Wilmington* (Philadelphia: T.K. Collins, Jr., 1851), p. 116. In 1759 Acrelius had written that, "The church at Christina usually held its services in Christina fort," *History of New Sweden* (1874 trans.), p. 176.
19. *SS*1:chapter 12; C. A. Weslager, *New Sweden on the Delaware*, pp. 61-66.
20. When the *Kalmar Nyckel* returned, Kling and Huygen learned that a vessel called the *Freedenburgh*, with the permission of the Swedish government, had taken Dutch farmers from Utrecht to New Sweden to enlarge the colony. Joost van den Bogaert was in charge of what Johnson terms the "Third Expedition," *SS* 1:135-144. The details are very vague, and if a settlement was made along the Delaware it was short-lived.

21. See Weslager, *New Sweden on the Delaware*, pp. 70-71 for the names as recorded in the Royal Archives, *SS* 1:151-53.
22. John H. Wuorinen, *The Finns on the Delaware* (New York: Columbia University Press, 1938).
23. C. A. Weslager, *The English on the Delaware* (New Brunswick: Rutgers University Press, 1967), chapter 7.
24. *SS* 1:155.
25. *Ibid.*, p. 156.
26. *Ibid.*, p. 240.
27. Sten Carlsson, "Three Swedish Expeditions to North America 1642-49," *Swedish American Genealogist* 8:24-26, 1988.
28. *SS* 1:244.
29. Carlsson, *ibid.*, p. 19.
30. *SS* 1:244-45. Weslager, *New Sweden on the Delaware*, p. 87.
31. Alf Åberg, *The People of New Sweden* (Stockholm: Natur Och Kultur, 1988). pp. 56-57.
32. *Instruction for Printz*, p. 159. Captain Hopp's list indicating that Papegoja and Walle Looer were passengers on the *Kalmar Nyckel* is found in Carlsson, *ibid.*, p. 24. On October 25, 1643, the government provided Papegoja with 60 D. for travel expenses, *SS* 1:243. The writer is unable to explain why Governor Printz made no reference to the arrival of the *Kalmar Nyckel*.
33. *Ibid.*, p. 105. Johnson states that adverse winds delayed the *Fama's* departure until June 20, *ibid.*, n.2.
34. *SS* 1:247.
35. *NYCD 1:143; SS* 1:247.
36. *NYCD* 1:159-60.
37. *Ibid.*, p. 156. Confirming data that the *Kalmar Nyckel* came to New Sweden (Virginia) on her fourth voyage is found in two letters written by the *Kalmar Nyckel's* ship's scribe are quoted in the *Appendix* below. Michell Johansson's statements are also supported by a pass issued

to him dated Sept.2, 1646, following his discharge, by Admirals Ryning and Gyllenhielm. Dr. Hulan who examined the original pass in the Krigsarkivet in Stockholm advises me that that it reads that Johansson made "two voyages to Virginia," and there can be no doubt that one of these was the 1643-1645 voyage on the *Kalmar Nyckel, Admiralitetskollegii registrur*, Sept. 2, 1646, p.732.

9. A Bitter Victory

War between Denmark and Sweden had been under way for almost a year when the *Kalmar Nyckel* and the *Fama* docked at Harlingen as they returned from their American voyage. A major naval battle had already been fought at Femern in Kiel Bay on October 16, 1644, which was an important victory for Sweden.[1] However, it did not end the war, and Sweden needed additional warships to finish the struggle. As soon as the *Kalmar Nyckel* and *Fama* discharged their cargoes, they were both commissioned for war duty. The records available to the writer do not provide information about what changes were made in the officer personnel, but it is a matter of record that a number of sailors from both vessels deserted at Harlingen.[2] Whether this was due to their opposition to war service, or for other reasons, is uncertain.

Distrust between Sweden and Denmark dated back to the Middle Ages followed by years of rivalry and an uneasy peace between the two powers. Hostility became intensified during the latter years of the Thirty Years' War as Sweden's strength grew in the Baltic where Denmark maintained an active political and economic presence. The territory Sweden occupied in Germany, and her then friendly relations with Holland, constituted a latent challenge to King Christian IV of Denmark. Conversely the Swedish government resented Denmark's possession of what are now the southern provinces of Sweden, and her control of the Öresund where Swedish vessels were compelled to pay tolls to the Danes for permission to sail through the sound. This was both a military and economic hindrance, inasmuch as water transportation between Sweden's two largest cities, Stockholm and Gothenburg, required unimpeded passage through the Öresund. See Map 3.

These and related subjects dealing with the Swedish-Danish War of 1643-45 are fully discussed in Swedish histories and are beyond the purview of this account.[3] Recognizing the importance of the war to Sweden, the writer was curious to learn whether or not the *Kalmar Nyckel* saw action in battles against the Danes. An affirmative answer is found in Sweden's military records.

The vessel, in fact, was directly involved in engagements leading to the ultimate defeat of the Danes. One war history provides the information that Admiral Mårten Thijsen Anckarhielm, who commanded the Swedish West Coast Fleet based at Gothenburg, accompanied by Vice Admiral Henrik Gerretsen, arranged to take the *Kalmar Nyckel* and *Fama* from Harlingen to Gothenburg to join the fleet. It appears that the two naval officers were then in Holland seeking Dutch assistance, and in addition to the two pinnaces, they brought back from Holland five "Louis de Geer ships" to join the Swedish fleet.[4] Louis de Geer, a wealthy Dutchman prominent in the iron business in Sweden, made a large number of ships available to the Swedish government for service during the war at his own expense.

Admiral Anckarhielm also engaged Dutch sea captains and experienced mates to enter Swedish service to man the new ships added to the fleet. On or about May 3, 1645 the contingent of men and ships from Holland arrived at Gothenburg where the *Kalmar Nyckel* and *Fama* were outfitted for battle duty. This probably meant taking aboard additional armament, gunners, and sailors to replace those who had deserted in Holland. Admiral Anckarhielm then made a tactical disposition of his forces retaining certain vessels at Gothenburg, and transferring others to Stockholm under Vice Admiral Gerretsen's command.[5]

Anckarhielm ordered the *Kalmar Nyckel* to remain with the naval forces at Gothenburg, and she was ready for action when the admiral received the alarming message in late May that a Danish fleet of some 16 to 20 warships was entering the inlet at Gothenburg at the mouth of the Gota River, and some vessels had already anchored at Galt Island. Once the enemy vessels were sighted, the admiral issued orders for the most effective positioning of his fleet of 13 vessels to protect the city. Before the Swedish ships could close in and engage the Danes in battle, a sudden southwestern storm blew up on May 24, and in the darkened skies the Danes were at a disadvantage in unfamiliar waters where numerous small rocky islands constituted a navigational hazard. A Danish pinnace scouting the islets was captured by the *Fama* and brought to Gothenburg.

The Danish flagship *Santa Sofia*, carrying 54 guns, was severely damaged. She sank, losing 15 men, after the storm forced her onto a rock. Admiral Ove Gjedde and the remainder of the crew were rescued, but the admiral ordered his ships to withdraw. When the storm clouds lifted, the Danish warships menacing the city had disappeared having sailed away as quietly as they appeared.[6] Admiral Anckarhielm did not know whether the enemy was setting a trap to lure him into the Skattegat straits, or whether they were hugging the southwest coast of Halland, then part of Danish territory, preparing to launch another sally on Gothenburg. The *Kalmar Nyckel* had a reputation as a swift vessel, and the admiral ordered her and another fast craft to spy on the enemy.

In their eagerness to obtain intelligence about the enemy's

movements, both ships, aided by favorable winds, traveled under full sail, and made contact sooner than their captains expected. Four of the Danish vessels broke away from their formation to attack the Swedish ships. Recognizing they were outnumbered, the two Swedish captains reversed their courses, and attempted to retreat to Gothenburg to report what they had learned, but the Danish vessels prevented them from doing so. The *Kalmar Nyckel* headed toward a strait which was then known, and is still called, the Great Baelt. After several hours of exchanging fire with the pursuing Danish ships, the *Kalmar Nyckel*, due to her speed, and the skill of her captain and crew, managed to escape and return to Gothenburg. So far as is known she and the companion vessel suffered no casualties in the *Kalmar Nyckel's* first contact with the enemy in the Danish War, but she certainly bore battle scars from the enemy's cannon.

Following the *Kalmar Nyckel's* return to Gothenburg she participated in the movements of the fleet, and was repositioned with other vessels at Stockholm preparing for battle in the south Baltic area. On July 7, 1645 she was under General Karl Gustav Wrangel's command at Bornholm, a small Danish island in the Baltic about 25 miles off the southern tip of Skåne (also owned by Denmark) where Swedish ships were assembling for action. General Wrangel ordered the *Kalmar Nyckel* and a ship called *Kattan (The Cat)* to sail to Falsterbo reef off the mainland diagonally south of Copenhagen, to scout and spy on the enemy. See Map 6. They were ordered to sail from there to Rügen (Dornbusch) with the intelligence they gathered, and rendezvous with the main Swedish fleet gathering off the present German coast in preparation for a major assault on Denmark.

On July 23, 1645, Admiral Erik Ryning, who had been given command of the fleet, divided the total force of 40 vessels into three squadrons. He took command aboard the *Scepter* in the first squadron which consisted of 14 ships, one of which

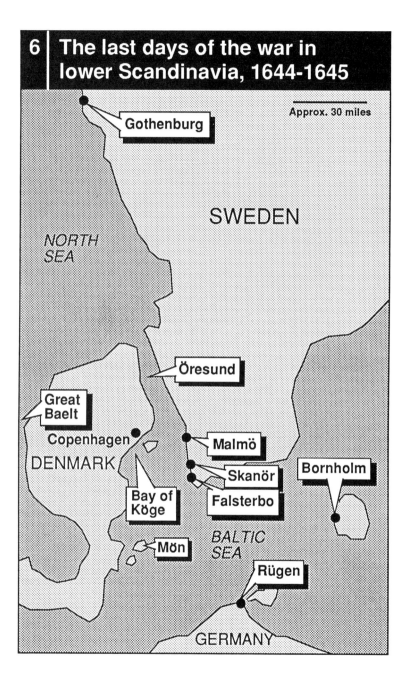

6 The last days of the war in lower Scandinavia, 1644-1645

Approx. 30 miles

Gothenburg

SWEDEN

NORTH SEA

Öresund

Great Baelt

Copenhagen

Malmö

DENMARK

Skanör

Bornholm

Bay of Köge

Falsterbo

Mön

BALTIC SEA

Rügen

GERMANY

Admiral Klas Fleming's flagship, the *Scepter*, which carried 346
soldiers and sailors and 56 cannon. After his death it became the
leading ship in Admiral Ryning's squadron in which the *Kalmar
Nyckel* was a spy ship during the Danish War of 1643-1645. (Reproduced from a work by Jacob Hägg (1839-1931), one of Sweden's
foremost marine artists.)

was the *Kalmar Nyckel*. General Wrangel was given command of the second squadron, also consisting of 14 vessels. It may seem odd that the admiralty placed a general in this position, but his squadron also carried cavalry and infantrymen fully armed to attack the enemy by land. Admiral Ake Ulfsparre commanded the third squadron consisting of 12 vessels, one of which was the *Cat*. Each of these 40 vessels, whose names are all on record, carried a number of cannon ranging from 12 to 66, giving the fleet a total firing power of 1,070 cannon, and a force of 5,900 sailors and soldiers.[7] With this formidable attacking force Admiral Ryning planned an offensive on land and sea with the objective of quickly ending the war with a Swedish victory.

The fleet sailed northeast to Mön, and on July 24, Admiral Ryning summoned his top commanders to a council of war on the *Scepter* for final orders. The next day the whole fleet went further north anchoring in the Bay of Köge from which they could see the Danish fleet in port at Copenhagen about 15 kilometers north of them. On August 6, with the Danish fleet awaiting an attack on Copenhagen, Admiral Ryning went aboard the *Kalmar Nyckel*, and General Wrangel boarded the *Swan* to confer with commanders of the army at Skanör. See Map 6. Plans were made and approved for General Wrangel to attack the islands in the Great Baelt by landing cavalry and infantry. Ryning then dispatched orders to Admiral Anckarhielm at Gothenburg to move his fleet south to lend support to General Wrangel in the Great Baelt.

Before Ryning returned to the *Scepter* lying at anchor in the Bay of Köge, the *Kalmar Nyckel* became engaged in battle on August 8 with the Danish ship named *St. Peter*, sometimes abbreviated to *St. Peer*. The Danish vessel was of a class known as a flöjten (flute) and she was well-armed with 22 cannon having fire power in excess of the *Kalmar Nyckel's* armaments, and the Danish crew was larger. Michell Johansson of Stockholm who had been aboard the *Kalmar Nyckel* as a clerk on her final voyage to New Sweden remained aboard at Harlingen and participated in the subsequent naval engagements. He was badly wounded in the battle with the *St. Peer,* and later wrote two letters to the Swedish king about the engagement and complained that pay was still owed him for his naval service. He states in one letter that members of the Swedish crew boarded the enemy ship, which means that the vessels pulled alongside each other for hand-to-hand encounter. Johansson does not say how many men were aboard the *Kalmar Nyckel,* but he states that only 12 officers and men survived the bloody encounter.[9] Both letters have been translated in the *Appendix* below. Other Swedish vessels helped the *Kalmar Nyckel* capture the *St. Peer.*

Admiral Ryning returned to the main fleet to signal the final assault, which had been thoroughly planned and coordinated. Suddenly the situation changed. On the morning of August 13, a courier brought him a high-priority dispatch from Chancellor Oxenstierna ordering him to cease hostilities. The Danes evidently recognized that resistance was useless, and agreed to negotiate peace terms. Ryning promptly sent a message to Admiral Anckarhielm ordering him to hold his flotilla at Gothenburg because victory was at hand.

Orders from Swedish and Danish commanders silenced the guns and cannon. Sweden had won a significant victory. Denmark ceded Gotland and Ösel to Sweden, and was compelled to give up important naval bases. Although Danish-Swedish rivalry had not permanently ended, the war proved to be a turning point in the 80 years of contention between the two powers for supremacy in the Baltic. With many impediments removed, Sweden was free to forge ahead and become a more powerful nation. Many lives were lost on both sides during the war, including one of Sweden's great leaders who had been an ardent supporter of Peter Minuit and the New Sweden colony — Admiral Klas Fleming. He was killed aboard his flagship by a stray bullet from a Danish battery.[10]

After the fighting ceased, the *Kalmar Nyckel*, still in need of repairs from her engagement with the *St. Pe(t)er*, was one of seven vessels ordered to return to Gothenburg in August of 1648.[11] Among these ships was the *Cat*, which had been a member of Admiral Ulfsparre's squadron, and was still carrying 20 guns and 97 soldiers and sailors.[12] Like the *Kalmar Nyckel*, the *Cat* had been damaged by enemy fire, but evidently to a lesser extent. The nature of the damage sustained by the two vessels is not given in detail in any accounts available to the writer, but the following exchange of communications suggest the *Kalmar Nyckel* was in worse condition than the *Cat*.

Governor Johan Printz in New Sweden had been clamoring for supplies and reinforcements because he had received no aid from the homeland during the war to help him to counter Dutch West India Company incursions along the Delaware. With the war ended, the directors of the company requested that the Swedish government equip the *Kalmar Nyckel*, and outfit her with soldiers and provisions so that assistance could be sent to Printz.[13] The request was made in Queen Christina's presence, and she gave her approval. The directors were not then aware of the sorry plight of the *Kalmar Nyckel*, and when they learned about her condition, they withdrew the request. The admiralty confirmed that the vessel was then about 20 years old and in no condition for another transatlantic voyage without undergoing expensive overhauling. The queen accordingly deferred to the company's wishes, and on April 13, 1649 issued the following directive to the admiralty, which has been translated into English for the first time by Dr. Richard H. Hulan:

> Our particular favor, gracious will and inclination in God almighty. We intended quite lately, by letters that have gone out to you, Lords Admirals and various Assessors in the Board of the Admiralty, to give you orders and command that you should make ready and equip the *Calmar Nyckel*,[14] which is lying at Gothenburg, and provide it with necessary people and munitions, so that now, this summer, and

the sooner the better, it could make a voyage to New Sweden, because the company's directors have most humbly made application
about this in our presence.

But in the meanwhile, on the contrary, the aforementioned directors have let it be known that the said ship, the *Calmar Nyckel*, will
not at this time be fit and serviceable for such a voyage; and we, all
the same, considering this to an extraordinary degree as a debt,
would delight also in seeing that the folk in New Sweden may be
relieved in time with one and another necessity:

Wherefore we graciously direct you, that without any delay you
permit the company to receive for that voyage another serviceable
ship, either [among] those that now are at Gothenburg, or that lie
here at Stockholm. Thereby you comply with our gracious will. God
guiding you by grace. From Stockholm the 13th of April 1649.[15]

CHRISTINA

The admiralty selected the *Cat* in lieu of the *Kalmar Nyckel*
to go to New Sweden, and Admiral Anckarhielm ordered her
to be put into condition for her first American voyage. She set
sail on July 3, 1649 with a large number of colonists, supplies
for New Sweden, and trade goods for Governor Printz to use
in bartering with the Indians.

Arriving in Caribbean waters, the *Cat* ran aground on sunk-
en reefs, and subsequently the passengers and crew experienced the worst catastrophe of all the expeditions sent to the
colony. They found temporary haven on a small uninhabited
island. Deprived of drinking water for eight days, the frightened
men, women, and children were exposed to a blistering sun,
probably sheltered by makeshift tents made from the ship's
sails. When a small bark passed the island, the crew fired
distress signals, which were later answered by the appearance
of two Spanish vessels. The Spaniards had no sympathy for
the Swedes primarily because of religious differences. They
looted the *Cat* of everything they could salvage before the
waves could batter her into a mass of rubble. The Spanish
vessels carried passengers and crew to Puerto Rico where they
were abused and robbed of personal belongings and clothing.
Some went from Puerto Rico to nearby islands where they
were also mistreated by the French. None of the members of

the expedition reached New Sweden, and only a handful survived the hardship and torture, and eventually got back to Sweden.[16]

The *Kalmar Nyckel* was spared the inglorious fate of the *Cat* due to the directors' fear that she could not withstand the long voyage, and the admiralty's reluctance to incur the expense of making the necessary repairs. The decision may have been a reasonable one from their point of view in light of the ship's years of exposure to raging seas, tempests, and the wear and tear of four voyages to America, climaxed by service in a bloody war in the Baltic. The admirals may have calculated that it was more economical in the long run to invest in a new ship instead of patching up an old one. Although the *Kalmar Nyckel* had served her country well in times of war and peace, a realistic decision had to be made, not on sentiment, but on her future usefulness as a ship of the line in the Swedish navy.

The admiralty recommended that the *Kalmar Nyckel* be offered for sale in the open market. This was not an unusual practice in the 17th century in Sweden, and other old ships were sold both to foreign nations and private buyers for possible reclamation. The final decision was made by Queen Christina herself, as authorized by the following royal document, also translated into English by Dr. Hulan:

> Christina by the Grace of God, Queen of Sweden, of the Goths and Wends, Grand Duchess of Finland, Duchess of Estonia, Karelia, Bremen, Verden, Stettin-Pomerania, Kashubia and Wenden, Princess of Rügen, Dame of Ingermanland and Wismar.
>
> Conveying Our particular favor and gracious disposition, in God almighty. Inasmuch as We, with faithful men and servants the Lords Admiral and the whole Council of the Admiralty, have granted Cornelius Rolofsson indulgence to buy the ship the *Calmar Nyckel* with its tackle; It is in accord with Our gracious will, that you may permit him to receive it for a reasonable price. And may God almighty commend you with particular grace. From Stockholm the 19th of June in the year 1651.
>
> [signed] CHRISTINA[17]

The letter in the Swedish language bearing Christina's signature authorizing the Swedish Admiralty to sell the *Kalmar Nyckel* in 1651 after 22 years of naval service. (Courtesy Swedish Royal Archives, Stockholm)

By a flourish of her quill pen Queen Christina decommissioned the *Kalmar Nyckel* retiring the ship from service in the Swedish government. The admiralty concurred that the vessel was worn out and no longer useful to the fleet without undergoing prohibitive expenses.

Who was Cornelius Rolofsson named in the queen's edict as the individual she approved to purchase the ship? His motives are unknown, because to date the writer has found no other reference to him in the Swedish records. A leading Swedish historian equally puzzled by Rolofsson's identity has suggested that it is possible he may have been a Dane, a Norwegian, or even a Dutchman.[18] If so, he could have officially represented a foreign government who believed the expense of restoring the vessel was justified. On the other hand, he may have personally bought the ship with the intention of renovating her for limited private use in local commerce.

The *Kalmar Nyckel* may then have ended her days sunken in the harbor of either a Swedish or foreign port after she was restored to service. Or a new owner may have dismantled her in order to salvage her ropes, timbers, canvas, spars, and masts. One thing seems evident: after the sale was consummated, the Swedish government did not try to preserve her memory by building a new *Kalmar Nyckel*.

Answers to some of the questions would permit adding a final note to the *Kalmar Nyckel's* long years of valiant service. But such answers could neither add nor detract from the career of the vessel which brought the first Swedes and Finns to Wilmington in the pioneer voyage of 1637-38, and returned with additional settlers in three subsequent voyages across a hazardous ocean. This has all been previously described in the above chapters.

One need only glance at the modern map on the following page to realize that the little colony Minuit founded in the Delaware estuary later grew into an area of 13,000 square miles of real estate of inestimable value. The Delaware estuary, composed of the bay and that part of the river affected by the tides, begins at Cape May and Cape Henlopen and ends at Trenton where the rapids, referred to as "the Falls" in early accounts, marked the break between the coastal plain and higher land. The Swedish government controlled the estuary for only a short period of time because New Sweden lost its political identity in the Dutch conquest of 1655, and the English conquered the Dutch nine years later.

This does not mean that the Scandinavians then returned to Europe; in choosing between their homeland and their new

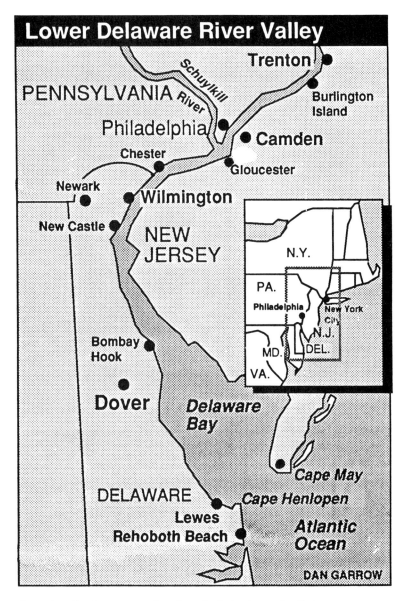

Lower Delaware River Valley

PENNSYLVANIA

Schuylkill River

Trenton

Burlington Island

Philadelphia

Camden

Chester

Gloucester

Newark

Wilmington

NEW JERSEY

New Castle

N.Y.

PA.

Philadelphia

New York City

N.J.

MD.

DEL.

VA.

Bombay Hook

Dover

Delaware Bay

Cape May

DELAWARE

Cape Henlopen

Lewes

Rehoboth Beach

Atlantic Ocean

DAN GARROW

Intentionally drawn out of scale to include the entire Delaware estuary, this map depicts the heart of New Sweden as of today. For a detailed map showing towns, cities, and all waterways drawn to scale see *The Delaware Estuary: Rediscovering a Forgotten Resource*, ed. Tracy L. Bryant and Jonathan R. Pennock (Newark: University of Delaware, Sea Grant College, 1988), op. p. 7.

homes, the vast majority remained in the Delaware valley. They had nothing to gain by returning to Europe, and good reasons for staying where they were. Some of the descendants of passengers who came over on the *Kalmar Nyckel's* voyages are residents more than 350 years later of towns and cities in the Delaware valley. Some are members of Dutch and Swedish Colonial Societies whose aim is to keep their heritage alive.

An influx of peoples of many nationalities, and different races and religions increased the total population of the former New Sweden. Delaware Bay and River continued to be an entrance for these people from all parts of the world. Today they make up a pluralistic society of 7.5 million people living in the Delaware valley south of Trenton. Some live and work in the urbanized north, and others farm the fertile fields in other parts of the watershed. The river and bay became a convenient boundary line between the states of Delaware and New Jersey; and the river between New Jersey and Pennsylvania. Certain parts of the estuary offer a vacationland, pleasant beaches, and a delight for sportsmen.

This great river system molded men and helped to create what Professor Thomas A. Bailey called "The American Spirit." The phrase is remindful that the New Sweden of the 17th century encompassed what later became the *first three states* to ratify the United States Constitution in the order named, Delaware, Pennsylvania, and New Jersey. These states not only constituted the heart of New Sweden as visualized by Peter Minuit, but they were the backbone of the 13 original American colonies.

Chapter 9 Notes

1. Börjesen, Hj. T. *Stockholms segelsjöfart: Minnesskrift 1732-1932* [Stockholm's Shipping by Sail] (Stockholm: Memorial Publication, 1932), p. 290 incorrectly states that the *Kalmar Nyckel* participated in the sea battle at Femern. She was then in the Atlantic returning from America.
2. Carlsson, "Three Swedish Expeditions," p. 7 states that Captain Hopp recorded 18 desertions from the *Kalmar Nyckel* at Harlingen and seven from the *Fama*.
3. For example, see Ingvar Anderson, *A History of Sweden*, trans. Carolyn Hannay (Stockholm: Natur Och Kultur, 1962, 4th printing.)
4. *Göteborg's Eskader Och Orlogsstation 1523-1870* [A History Compiled and Published by the Defense Department's Warhistorical Department] (Göteborg, 1949), pp. 42-43. The writer gratefully acknowledges the assistance of Marianne Eckerström Mackenzie for translating relevant passages from this volume.
5. *Ibid.*, p. 42.
6. *Ibid.*, p. 43.

7. Axel Zettersten, *Svenska Flottans Historia* [History of the Swedish Navy] (Norrtelje: Norrtelje Tidnings Boktryskeri, vol. 2, 1903), pp. 376-77. The English translations were also made by Mrs. Mackenzie. The author is indebted to Patricia Thatcher for photocopying pertinent passages of this book at the Library of Congress.
8. *Ibid.*, p. 377.
9. *SS* 1:251. Cf. Johansson's letters in *Appendix* below. For evidence that Johansson was aboard the *Kalmar Nyckel*, see Carlsson, *ibid.*, pp. 19, 22.
10. *Ibid.*, 2:680.
11. *Göteborg's Eskader*, p. 13. Prior to returning to Gothenburg, the *Kalmar Nyckel* was given a number of important assignments, one of which was to take Major General Erik Stenbock to Riga, and from there to transport the Chancellor of the Exchequer, Gabriel Bengston Oxenstierna, and his party back to Stockholm. Zettersten, p. 383. The latter, an important government official, had been one of the original investors in the New Sweden Company.
12. Zettersten, p. 377.
13. *SS* 1:267.
14. The queen used the early spelling of Kalmar, but a K instead of a C is preferred modern usage.
15. The author is indebted to the National Archives, Stockholm for a photocopy of this document.
16. An account of the *Cat's* voyage is given in *SS* 1:269-276, although Johnson errs in stating that one of the passengers, Timen Stiddem with his wife and five children, managed to return to Amsterdam, p. 276. Research conducted by Dr. Richard H. Hulan indicates that Stiddem's first wife and three small children lost their lives in Puerto Rico. He later remarried and returned to New Sweden.
17. The author is indebted to the National Archives, Stockholm for a copy of this document.
18. Dr. Sten Carlsson, personal letter March 18, 1989.

APPENDIX

Settlers Arriving On the *Kalmar Nyckel* - 1640

The *Kalmar Nyckel* did not bring any women or children to New Sweden in 1638, and when it sailed back to Sweden it left 25 men at Fort Christina. Most of them returned to Sweden when the vessel arrived on the second voyage, and no official record was made of the few that remained.[1] The following list of names, compiled by Peter S. Craig, leaves no doubt that women and children arrived on the second voyage; these were the first families to settle in the colony. The list is not complete, but it is the best that can now be offered and is subject to expansion. Although the majority remained in New Sweden as permanent settlers, some returned to Sweden on ships that later delivered new colonists. Moreover, some who returned to Sweden came back again to the colony. Where the occupation and place of origin is known this information is shown alongside the name.

Peter Hollender Ridder, commander, Ekenäs, Nyland, Finland
Joost van Langdonk, commissary, Dutch
Gregorius van Dyck, assistant commissary, Dutch
The Reverend Reorus Torkillus, pastor
William Loury, provost
Johan Michellsson, corporal
Anders Jönsson, gunner
Bengt Thomasson, soldier

Anders Nilsson Nagell, soldier
Olof Svensson, soldier
Steffan Olofsson, soldier
Nils Svensson, soldier
Peter Gunnarsson Rambo, Hisingen (Gothenburg)
Anders Svensson Bonde
Måns Anderson
    his wife
    his daughter, Brita
Jon Thorsson
Anders Larsson Dalbo
Sven Larsson Maarbo
Sven Gunnarsson
    his wife
    his son, Sven
    his daughter, Gertrude
    his son, Olof, born at sea[2]
Lars Svensson Bonde
Mårten Göttersson

Settlers Arriving On The *Kalmar Nyckel* or the *Charitas* - 1641

As discussed in the text, the *Kalmar Nyckel* and the *Charitas* traveled together on the *Kalmar Nyckel's* third voyage to New Sweden in 1641-42. On this expedition the names of some, but not all, of the passengers were recorded before the vessels left Sweden. However, there is no record at Gothenburg which lists the name of the ship to which each passenger was assigned. Peter S. Craig's documentary research permits identifying a few of the passengers assigned to one or the other vessel, but the majority must be listed as having sailed on either the *Kalmar Nyckel* or the *Charitas*. As with those shown on the above 1640 list the majority of these passengers remained in New Sweden as colonists, although some returned to Sweden on later vessels.

Those known to have arrived on the *Kalmar Nyckel*:
Mats Hansson, gunner
   his wife, Elizabeth
Laurens Andriessen, a Dutch "cuyper"
Olof Thorsson, sailor
   his wife, Elise
   his son, Lars
   his son, Olle
   his daughter, Christina
Mats Olofsson, sailor
Måns Jöransson, laborer, Finn

Those known to have arrived on the *Charitas*:
Måns Svensson Lom, freeman, from Roslagen
   his wife
   his daughter, Margaret
   his daughter, Catherine
   his son, Peter
Knut Mårtensson, sailor, Vasa, Finland
Lars Thomasson [Bure], sailor, from Veddige
Ifver Sifferson
Clas Classon, Dutch carpenter
Hendrick Huygen, commissary, from Wesel, Germany[3]
Gotfried Harmer, cabin guard, from Worms, Germany[4]

Those who arrived either on the *Charitas* or *Kalmar Nyckel*:
(The likelihood is that the majority were on the *Kalmar Nyckel* because the *Charitas* transported animals and fodder as well as supplies, and had only limited space for passengers.)
   Ivert Hendricksson, laborer, Finn
   Olof Pålsson, laborer
   Per Johansson, laborer
   Johan Ericksson, laborer, from Ångermanland
   Anders Hansson, laborer (brother to Mats Hansson above)
   Jacob Sprint, laborer, from Nyland

Påul Jönsson, laborer, from Jämtland
Axel Stille, laborer, from Roslagen
Hendrick Matsson, laborer
Johan Andersson [Stalcop], boy from Strängnis
Olof Erickson, a boy
Olof Stille, freeman, from Roslagen
  his wife
  his daughter, Ella
  his son, Anders
Mats Hansson, laborer, Borgå, Finland
Peter Larsson Kock, laborer, from Bångsta
Carl Johansson, Keksholm, Finland
Eskel Larsson, army deserter
Mr. Christopher, preacher
Gustaf Strahl
Mickel Jonsson Bolm, Reval, Estonia
Måns Nilsson Kling[5]
  his wife
  his small child
  his servant girl
Carl Markusson
Påfvel Schmal, boy from Norrmalm (Stockholm)
Jöran Olsson, provost
Peter Andersson, guard
Hans Månsson, laborer, from Skara
Lars Björnsson, sailor, Gothenburg
Anders Christiansson, miller, Gothenburg
Clement Jöransson, laborer, Finn from Sunne
Hendrick Matsson, laborer, Finn
Eskel Larsson, laborer, Finn from Sunne
Bartel Eskellson, laborer, Finn from Sunne
Jöns Påvelsson, laborer, Finn from Sunne

Michell Johansson's Undated Letters — Written c. 1662[6]

Most Powerful King
Most Gracious Lord

It is with great cause that I entreat Your Royal Majesty with this my most obsequious petition: most humbly making known, that I served under his Royal Majesty's and the Kingdom's Admiralty, as a ship's scribe; And during that time, several journeys to Virginia and the West Indies gave me occasion to serve, as my Pass from the most praiseworthy Royal Admiralty dated 2 September in the year 1646, hereto attached, shows; which, by immeasurable favor has been transmitted; On which journeys I suffered extreme hardship: in particular in the year 1645 on the 7th of August in the territory of Denmark; When the ship *Calmar Nyckel* boarded, with Denmark's ship named *St. Peer*, between Malmö and Copenhagen; no more remained alive of *Calmar Nyckel's* folk than 12 men, of officers and common men; There I, poor man, was shot and crippled: God mend it. Now, in my need and great poverty, I have to live with a paralyzed body, over which may he himself (God) take pity. And on account of all that, most humbly petitioning, I hereby wish to have a plea made, about the restoration of my wages. For the year 1645, when I came to Stockholm, on the 8th of November, I received 14 daler 25 1/2 öre silvermint, as the ledgers maintained by the regiment's scribe, the late Daniel Martensson, show, so much to be delivered to me from the Admiralty's cash account: Much more, both that and the Royal Admiralty's books clearly show, I have been due to collect for the years 1643, 1644, and 1645 up until the 8th of November: But after I entered into the service of the late paymaster Daniel Kock at the Western Iron Mining District, *I continued for 16 years' time on the job there*; so it was, that my claim was impeded, and my former comrades put their back wages to good use: I in humility made several demands to the Royal Admiralty, but to date, I have not been able to accomplish the slightest thing thereby. So much more confidently begging the pardon of your Royal Majesty's most gracious favour, which alleviates all the sufferings of the poor, more particularly the physically disabled, among whom I count myself one, who also have been the Crown's servant, and am now paralyzed, and have sailed on the Crown's ships both in the Eastern and Western Seas. May your Royal Majesty dispose everything out of Royal favor, and compassion; let me be worthy to receive my little wages, in my great poverty and paralysis. Wherefore I desire, with furor and fervent sighing, (God) cause your Royal Majesty to act most graciously and solace me in this my need, requested in distress; which may God repay, and I now, in the most faithful way, do fervently so pray.

> Your Royal Majesty's
> Most frail and broken down
> old servant,
> Michell Johansson, in times past
> Ship's Scribe on the ship
> *Calmar Nyckel* to the West Indies

> Most Powerful King
> Most Gracious Lord

Before your Royal Majesty's feet I, a poor old man and servant of the Crown, am indeed compelled most obsequiously to declare by means of this supplication, how as I have served for some time under the Royal Admiralty, and on the Crown's ships in the Baltic Sea, and was likewise given the duties of a Scribe to Virginia, until in the former Danish territories in the year 1645 I was wounded, so that I was no longer able to perform sea duties, as will be shown, to the letter, by the following copy of the Royal Admiralty's Pass, And have received no more wages for the years 1643, 1644, and 1645, than 14 Daler 25 1/2 öre silvermint, upon my homecoming the 8th of November in the last-named year, as the Royal Admiralty's books show: even though I have indeed for several years most humbly requested the outstanding balance of my back wages, so this my demand has been withheld, likewise even until this day: Now I am brought by this poor end into the very greatest need and poverty. Your Royal Majesty, on account of all this, I most humbly plead, in the frailty of my old age, for this: that your Royal Majesty be pleased to notice, with the most favorable consideration, my poor, faithful service, and old age, into which I have continued and persevered to the point of feebleness. Now most graciously, by Royal favor, bless me with a few grains for my last days, that my poor wife might be comforted by them: God almighty crown your Royal Majesty with a long life, good peaceful holiness and a happy reign. Hereupon I, a poor, elderly and frail man await your Royal Majesty's most gracious resolution.

> Your Royal Majesty's
> most obsequious, humble
> old servant,
> Michell Johansson, in times past
> Scribe on the ship
> *Calmar Nyckel* to Virginia[7]

Notes

1. A member in the first expedition named Clas Jansson remained as a freeman. The probability is that Timen Stiddem, the barber-surgeon, also remained and returned to Sweden in 1644 according to Governor Printz's Monatgelderbuch (Monthly Account Book). He apparently returned to the colony with Governor Rising in 1654, and remained permanently.
2. For evidence of his birth during the voyage, see *Peter*

Kalm's Travels in North America, trans. Adolph Benson (New York: Wilson-Ericson, 1937), p. 731.

3. The writer suggested in the text that Huygen's attachment to the colony may have subconsciously been influenced by the memory of his dead uncle, Peter Minuit. Returning for the second time, he remained through the Johan Printz administration (1643-1653) as the commissary and Indian trader; he also served as clerk of the court over which Printz presided. He returned to Sweden with Printz in 1653, and in 1655 he invested 3000 daler in the New Sweden Company then called the American Company (*SS* 2:626). He came back to America in 1656 on the *Mercurius*, as commander of the vessel and chief commissary-designate of the colony. To his surprise he found the Dutch in control. In later years he returned to Wesel, and in 1674, approximately aged 65, he became a citizen of Kleve. (Gorrisen, p. 116). No reference has been found to a wife or children.

4. Minuit's grandnephew, he became an assistant to Huygen, and remained to serve Printz who recommended him highly. However, he deserted the colony and settled in Maryland.

5. Kling must have been favorably impressed with the opportunities existing in New Sweden or he would not have returned bringing his family. However, he did not remain, but returned to Sweden in 1648 (*SS* 2:453).

6. Although Dr. Amandus Johnson was aware of the existence of both of these letters he did not make an English translation of either, and he made a palpable error by dating them both 1646, *SS* 1: n. 6, p. 251. Since Michell Johansson states he returned to Stockholm Nov. 8, 1645, and then found work in the Western Iron Mining District for 16 years (see italicized line) the letters could not possibly have been written prior to 1661. Johnson's confusion in the dates also negates his statement that the *Kalmar*

Nyckel did not come to New Sweden on her fourth voyage, *ibid.*, n. 18, p. 244 in view of the contents of the letters.

7. As previously discussed, Virginia was frequently used by the Swedes in referring to New Sweden, but never to the Caribbean Islands. Michell Johansson had obviously been to both places. The English translations of both of the above letters were made by Dr. Richard H. Hulan.

INDEX

(Note: names in the unnumbered 16-page pictorial insert are not indexed)

Grants from The Crystal Trust and ICI Americas made the
publication and distribution of this book possible.
Their contribution is hereby gratefully acknowledged.